craft **workshop**

polymer clay

craft **workshop**

polymer clay

The art of clay modelling in over 25 beautiful projects

Mary Maguire

Photography by Steve Dalton

southwater

For Rebecca, Beatrice, Deirdre, Scott, Arron and Marion

THIS EDITION IS PUBLISHED BY SOUTHWATER

SOUTHWATER IS AN IMPRINT OF ANNESS PUBLISHING LTD
HERMES HOUSE, 88–89 BLACKFRIARS ROAD, LONDON SE1 8HA
TEL. 020 7401 2077; FAX 020 7633 9499
WWW.SOUTHWATERBOOKS.COM; INFO@ANNESS.COM

© ANNESS PUBLISHING LTD 1996, 2003

UK AGENT: THE MANNING PARTNERSHIP LTD,
6 THE OLD DAIRY, MELCOMBE ROAD, BATH BA2 3LR;
TEL. 01225 478 444; FAX 01225 478 440;
SALES@MANNING-PARTNERSHIP.CO.UK

UK DISTRIBUTOR: GRANTHAM BOOK SERVICES LTD,
ISAAC NEWTON WAY, ALMA PARK INDUSTRIAL ESTATE,
GRANTHAM, LINCS NG31 9SD;
TEL. 01476 541080; FAX 01476 541061;
ORDERS@GBS.TBS-LTD.CO.UK

NORTH AMERICAN AGENT/DISTRIBUTOR: NATIONAL
BOOK NETWORK, 4501 FORBES BOULEVARD,
SUITE 200, LANHAM, MD 20706;
TEL. 301 459 3366; FAX 301 429 5746;
WWW.NBNBOOKS.COM

AUSTRALIAN AGENT/DISTRIBUTOR: PAN MACMILLAN
AUSTRALIA, LEVEL 18, ST MARTINS TOWER,
31 MARKET ST, SYDNEY, NSW 2000;
TEL. 1300 135 113; FAX 1300 135 103;
CUSTOMER.SERVICE@MACMILLAN.COM.AU

A CIP CATALOGUE RECORD FOR THIS BOOK IS AVAILABLE
FROM THE BRITISH LIBRARY.

PUBLISHER: JOANNA LORENZ
PROJECT EDITOR: JUDITH SIMONS
PHOTOGRAPHER: STEVE DALTON
DESIGNER: ROGER WALKER AND
GRAHAM HARMER
STYLIST: SUE PITMAN
ILLUSTRATORS: VANA HAGGERTY AND MADELEINE DAVID

PREVIOUSLY PUBLISHED AS *NEW CRAFTS POLYMER CLAYWORK*

10 9 8 7 6 5 4 3 2 1

PICTURE ACKNOWLEDGEMENTS
Page 8, by kind permission of the Trustees of the British Museum, page 15 (left) George Post.

CONTENTS

INTRODUCTION

P OLYMER CLAY IS A VERSATILE, EASY TO HANDLE MODELING MEDIUM THAT CAN BE USED FOR MAKING OBJECTS AS DIVERSE AS ORNATE JEWELRY, MINIATURE TEA SETS, DOLLS, TOY THEATERS, LAMPS, TABLEWARE AND MIRROR FRAMES. KNOWN TO DOLL AND MODEL MAKERS FOR SEVERAL DECADES, THIS REMARKABLE MATERIAL IS NOW WIDELY AVAILABLE FOR ANYONE TO USE, AND NEW TECHNIQUES ARE BEING DEVELOPED ALL THE TIME.

SIMILAR IN SOME WAYS TO ORDINARY CLAY, POLYMER CLAY HAS MANY ADVANTAGES. IT IS MADE IN A WIDE RANGE OF COLORS, INCLUDING FLUORES-CENT AND GLOW-IN-THE-DARK, AND COLORS CAN BE MIXED OR JUXTAPOSED TO CREATE SOME AMAZINGLY INTRICATE EFFECTS. IT DOES NOT SHRINK, MAK-ING IT SUITABLE FOR EMBEDDING OBJECTS, AND ONCE BAKED IT IS WATER-PROOF AND DURABLE. IN ADDITION, POLYMER CLAY CAN BE TREATED WITH SHINY METALLIC FINISHES.

ALL YOU NEED TO WORK WITH POLYMER CLAY ARE YOUR HANDS, A CRAFT KNIFE, A KITCHEN TABLE AND AN ORDINARY DOMESTIC OVEN, ALTHOUGH MORE SPECIALIZED TOOLS WILL BE NECESSARY FOR MORE ADVANCED TECH-NIQUES. THE TECHNIQUES REQUIRED ARE STRAIGHTFORWARD AND EASY TO LEARN, AND ONCE YOU HAVE ACQUIRED THE BASIC SKILLS AND MADE SOME OF THE MORE ADVANCED PROJECTS SHOWN IN THIS BOOK, YOU WILL BE ABLE TO CREATE YOUR OWN PROJECTS AND DESIGNS AND PERHAPS EVEN ACHIEVE THE LEVEL OF CRAFTSMANSHIP ILLUSTRATED IN THE GALLERY SECTION.

Left: Polymer clay can be used to create a dazzling array of colorful objects, from simple buttons to quirky cutlery and eye-catching decorations for the home.

HISTORY OF POLYMER CLAY

POLYMER CLAY ORIGINATED IN GERMANY IN THE LATE 1930S. IT WAS AN ACCIDENTAL CHEMICAL BY-PRODUCT THAT WAS DISCOVERED BY MRS REHBINDER, THE DAUGHTER OF THE FAMOUS DOLL-MAKER KÄTHE KRUSE. DURING THE SECOND WORLD WAR SHE DID NOT HAVE A SUITABLE RAW MATERIAL FROM WHICH TO MAKE DOLLS' HEADS. SHE EXPERIMENTED WITH THIS BY-PRODUCT AND FOUND THAT IT COULD BE MODELED AND HARDENED IN AN OVEN. SHE CONTINUED TO EXPERIMENT WITH THE MATERIAL FOR SOME YEARS, USING IT TO CREATE MOSAICS, AS WELL AS FOR HER INITIAL PURPOSE OF DOLLS' HEADS. SHE DEVELOPED A LIMITED COLOR RANGE, WHICH SHE STARTED TO SELL UNDER THE NAME OF FIFI MOSAIK – DERIVED FROM HER NICKNAME FIFI AND ITS MOSAIC APPLICATION.

Until 1964 she marketed her product alone, without advertising. Then she approached Eberhard Faber and acquired a license for industrial production. The product is now sold as Fimo.

Sculpy, the American equivalent, was developed in the late 1960s by a company called Polyform products in Illinois. Other brands of polymer clay are mostly produced in Germany, such as Formello, Modello and Cermit. The production and quality of polymer clay have improved enormously in its sixty-year existence. Each brand of polymer clay has its own color range and they all differ in consistency and cooking directions.

Because its history is so recent, it is really still establishing and defining itself - and polymer clay artists tend to draw heavily on well-established techniques from other disciplines. The most popular of these are

Above: Cane work was used in Ancient Egypt to produce faces made from mosaic glass slices. The two slices here show an exaggerated expression on a male face, suggestive of a Greek mask.
Left: An example of the late medieval art of millefiori: a glass bead embellished with canes and traces of gilding.

cane work and millefiori, which are now undergoing a renaissance.

These partner arts of glassworking are thought to have developed in Mesopotamia, and quality works of great craftsmanship were being produced in Alexandria and ancient Egypt. The art was rediscovered by the Italians in the late fifteenth century. It was they who called it millefiori, which literally means a thousand flowers.

Cane work is used to make a batch of multiple images. Long colored rods of glass are placed next to each other to form a picture or pattern and fused together so that the picture runs through the length of the cane. Slices are taken from the cane at this point, or the picture or pattern can be miniaturized by a process called reduction – by rolling the molten canes they can be elongated, then sliced. These perfect little miniatures can be applied to the surface of a glass bead, under a hot flame. This process is known as lampwerk. The slices are fused onto the surface of the bead, side by side, until the bead is completely covered – hence millefiori.

It is an enchanting technique with various applications. Beads and paperweights made by Murona craftsmen, or those from the French company Campagne des Cristallenes de Baccavat are much sought after by collectors.

Polymer clay is ideally suited to this technique, and brings new dimensions to this art form. What it lacks in transparency it makes up for in its versatility and its wide range of colors. Polymer clay objects and jewelry are now attracting collectors in their own right.

Cane work and millefiori, ancient techniques in the art of glasswork, have proved to be extremely well-suited to the modern material of polymer clay. Left: In cane work, long rods of pictures are made, from which slices are taken. For the next stage of millefiori, above, the slices of cane are then used to completely cover a plain bead, providing diverse, intricate decoration. (Beads and picture canes by Ingrid Proudfoot.)

GALLERY

Although polymer clay has yet to be taken seriously by the art world at large, there is no doubt about its huge potential as an art medium, and exciting and innovative developments are occurring all the time. A growing number of artists have already recognized the unique properties of polymer clay and used them to develop their own particular styles and techniques. To inspire you to explore and experiment with this fascinating medium, some of these artists are featured here with examples of their work, which help to show the material's versatility and attraction.

Left: CITY ZEN CANE
David Forlano and Steven Ford trained as painters at the Tyler School of Art in Rome where they drew inspiration for their mosaic picture frames and eggs. Each design consists of thousands of tiny colored squares of various tints to make them look like ancient stone. The eggs are made by placing cane slices of real shells from blown-out duck and goose eggs. Founding members of the National Polymer Guild in the USA, both artists teach intermediate and advanced polymer clay workshops.
DAVID FORLANO &
STEVEN FORD

Below: HEART BROOCH
AND FLOWER JEWELRY
Lara Bohnic designs jewelry and also works as a product and fashion designer. Attracted by the lightness, color and easy workability of one of the softer of the polymer clays, she takes her inspiration from nature, pop art and kitsch culture.
LARA BOHNIC

Left: PEOPLE BEADS
These people beads are made by layering tiny pieces of polymer clay onto a basic bead then incorporating cane work into the costumes. Each bead is unique and takes anywhere from several hours to weeks to complete.
CYNTHIA TROOP

Below: PAPERWEIGHTS
Ingrid Proudfoot began experimenting with making polymer clay jewelry a decade ago and now makes various artifacts including buttons, door knobs, clocks and umbrella handles. She mainly uses cane work in which a strong African influence is detectable. Her beads and picture canes are also illustrated in the history section of this book.
INGRID PROUDFOOT

Below: IRIDESCENT EARRINGS
Mary Maguire has been making
polymer clay jewellery since 1986.
She prefers to use just one base
colour with a metal leaf applied to
the surface and likes to incorporate
shells and other found objects into
her work.
MARY MAGUIRE

Right: MINIATURE THEATRE
Theresa Pateman first started to
use polymer clay to make jewellery
but when she discovered its
versatility she began creating
figures around wire armature.
Inspired by a visit to the Musée
Grevin in Paris, a wax museum,
she devised the miniature theatre.
THERESA PATEMAN

Right: BROOCHES
These two brooches (pins) were made
using a technique adapted from the
Japanese metalworking art of *Mokume
Gane,* which usually consists of laminating
thin sheets of silver, gold and copper
alloy, fusing the layers together then
distorting the shape to create a watermark
or woodgrain pattern when sliced
through. This effect is much easier to
achieve with polymer clay by layering thin
slices of translucent clay, which have very
small amounts of colour mixed in, and
silver leaf. The block is then deformed to
create an uneven surface and thin slices
are taken off it. These are then collaged
onto the surface of a base shape.
LINDLY HAUNANI

Left: HAT PIN & JEWELLERY
Sandra Duvall and Julia Hill designed the hat pin, the three piece brooch and the brooch and earring set which are all made by the millefiori technique. They also specialize in buttons, hair slides, drop earrings, cufflinks and tie pins. They draw inspiration from Matisse and primitive decoration.
SANDRA DUVALL &
JULIA HILL

Left: CENTRAL PARK
The buildings in this dazzling picture of New York's Central Park are constructed from wood and the figures, trees and windows are made from polymer clay. The choice of bright colours captures the energy of the city.
KAREN KRIGE

Above: CLOCK JEWELLERY
Having previously been making jewellery for a decade, Eileen Mahony began using polymer clay in about 1990. Her soft watches are built up from three-dimensional layers of clay then guilded with bronze powders and the numerals painted on, influenced by Dali's painting *The Persistence of Memory*. She also makes psychedelic millefiori jewellery as well as small boxes and mirrors.
EILEEN MAHONY

Left: GILDED BROOCHES
Drawing from their
backgrounds in illustration
and ceramics, Eric Pateman
and Fiona French taught
themselves the art of
jewelry making. They lay
gold and silver leaf onto
polymer clay, then paint
the cooked pieces. Their
work has strong Celtic and
Egyptian flavors.
KITCHEN TABLE STUDIO

Left: BLACK AND GOLD CANDLESTICKS
Sarah Nelson Shriver makes jewelry and decorations out of polymer clay. These candlesticks are 10 inches high, with an interior vertical support of nylon-reinforced plastic tubing. The decorative elements were applied using the millefiori technique.
SARAH NELSON SHRIVER

Below: FACE PINS
Iridian Faces are vibrant character face pins created by Ellen Watt. She has been making the faces since 1989 and each one is unique. Ellen uses customized cookie cutters to form the basic shapes from polymer clay slabs. They are hand-manipulated from there.
ELLEN WATT

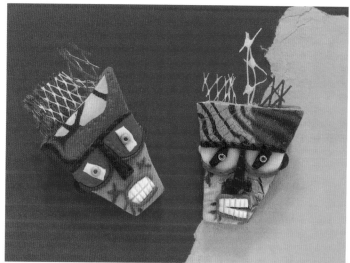

Left: HEARTS OF GOLD
Deborah Banyas and T. P. Speer are sculptors working with polymer clay. *Hearts of Gold* is constructed out of wood and stuffed cotton. The polymer clay was then applied and the piece finished in acrylic paint and gold leaf.
DEBORAH BANYAS &
T. P. SPEER

MATERIALS

POLYMER CLAY IS ACTUALLY A PLASTIC KNOWN AS POLYVINYL CHLORIDE. WITH ALL THE ADVANTAGES OF REAL CLAY, IT HAS NONE OF THE DISADVANTAGES. IT CAN BE MOLDED, MODELED, SCULPTED, STRETCHED AND EMBOSSED PRIOR TO BEING BAKED. IT IS CLEAN TO WORK WITH, IT DOES NOT SHRINK AND IT IS ALREADY COLORED, MAKING GLAZING OR PAINTING UNNECESSARY EXCEPT FOR CREATING DECORATIVE EFFECTS. IN ADDITION, IT DOES NOT REQUIRE FIRING AT HIGH TEMPERATURES, LIKE OTHER TYPES OF CLAY.

BAKING POLYMER CLAY IN AN ORDINARY DOMESTIC OVEN AT 215–275° F, ACCORDING TO THE MANUFACTURER'S INSTRUCTIONS, FUSES PARTICLES TOGETHER IN THE POLYMERIZATION PROCESS WHICH TRANSFORMS THE CLAY FROM A MALLEABLE SUBSTANCE INTO A SOLID ONE. ONCE BAKED, THE CLAY CAN BE SANDED, SAWN, DRILLED AND GLUED.

VARIOUS BRANDS OF POLYMER CLAY ARE SOLD. ALTHOUGH THEY ARE ALL BASICALLY THE SAME, SOME HAVE A SLIGHTLY DIFFERENT CONSISTENCIES AND SOME ARE MORE SPECIFICALLY DESIGNED AS ECONOMICAL MODELING CLAYS FOR MAKING DOLLS AND MODELS. EXPERIENCE WILL SOON TELL YOU WHICH TYPES OF POLYMER CLAY YOU PREFER FOR DIFFERENT TYPES OF PROJECTS.

THERE IS AN EVER-INCREASING RANGE OF COLORS AVAILABLE WHICH NOW INCLUDE STARTLING FLUORESCENT, PEARLESCENT, AND METALLIC COLORS AS WELL AS GLOW-IN-THE-DARK, TRANSPARENT AND MOTTLED STONE EFFECTS.

MOST MANUFACTURERS SELL THEIR CLAYS IN BLOCKS THAT WEIGH ABOUT 2 OUNCES BUT FOR ECONOMY, LARGER BLOCKS ARE AVAILABLE IN LIMITED COLOR RANGES AND OF THE SPECIALIZED MODELING CLAY.

Doll-making polymer clay is stiffer than most and is available in large blocks.

Modeling polymer clay is easier to work but stronger once baked and is available in large blocks.

Pearlescent polymer clay has a creamy sheen.

Translucent polymer clay can be used in a number of interesting ways.

Glow-in-the-dark polymer clay can be used to make items that show up in the dark.

Mix quick polymer clay is easy to work and suitable for use by children.

Mottled stone is an imitation stone effect that can be applied to polymer clay in a number of colors.

Glamour colors provide a metallic effect on polymer clay.

Softer polymer clay is available in a range of colors.

Fluorescent and ordinary colors are exciting and fun to use.

Epoxy resin glue is used in two parts and is very strong glue.

Aluminum wire can be used for building support structures.

Jewelry wire is used for connecting pieces for earrings and necklaces.

Metallic leaf in gold, silver, copper and aluminum is used for decorating the surface of clay.

Fridge magnets are produced by polymer clay manufacturers for use with their clays.

Button backs are useful for making clay buttons.

Barrettes can be decorated with clay beads or strips.

Beads and gemstones must be flat backed and, if they are to go into the oven, made of glass.

Clip-on earring backs and metal button backs are used to make jewelry pieces.

Bronze powders A limited range is produced by polymer clay manufacturers. A wide range of colors is available at artsuppy stores.

Varnish, gloss or matte, is supplied by polymer clay manufacturers.

Acrylic paint can be used for covering the surface of polymer clay.

Enamel paint is used for painting small areas or patterns.

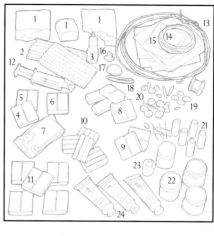

KEY

 1 Doll-making polymer clay
 2 Modeling polymer clay
 3 Diluent
 4 Pearlescent polymer clay
 5 Translucent polymer clay
 6 Glow-in-the-dark polymer clay
 7 Mix quick polymer clay
 8 Mottled stone effect
 9 Glamour colors
10 Softer polymer clay
11 Fluorescent and ordinary colors
12 Epoxy resin glue
13 Aluminum wire
14 Jewelry wire
15 Metallic leaf
16 Fridge magnets
17 Button back
18 Barrette
19 Beads and gemstones
20 Clip-on earring backs and metal button backs
21 Bronze powders (branded)
22 Bronze powders
23 Acrylic paint
24 Enamel paint

EQUIPMENT

IN ADDITION TO AN ORDINARY HOUSEHOLD OVEN, THE MOST IMPOR-
TANT TOOLS REQUIRED FOR WORKING WITH POLYMER CLAY ARE YOUR
HANDS. WHEN YOU FIRST START, HOUSEHOLD ITEMS GLEANED FROM
KITCHEN DRAWERS AND SEWING, KNITTING AND TOOL BOXES WILL DO.
PINS, KNITTING NEEDLES, CHEESE SLICERS, SCREWS, PENS AND EVEN
MATCHES CAN ALL BE IMPROVISED AS TOOLS, AND YOU WILL FIND THAT A
VARIETY OF OBJECTS CAN PRODUCE PATTERNS. BUT FOR MORE ADVANCED
WORK, MORE SPECIALIZED EQUIPMENT WILL BE USEFUL. WHATEVER
EQUIPMENT YOU USE FOR POLYMER CLAY, KEEP IT EXCLUSIVELY FOR THAT
PURPOSE AND NEVER USE IT FOR PREPARING FOOD.

Oven An oven is necessary for baking the clay at specified temperatures. For those who prefer not to place plastic materials in their domestic ovens, at least one polymer clay manufacturer markets a special oven.

Mirror Placed behind the work, a mirror will enable you to see all around when slicing large canes or blocks, ensuring neat, even cuts.

Oven thermometer Using an oven thermometer ensures that your oven is working at the correct temperature for the clay. This is important because undercooked clay can be fragile, and overcooking burns the clay.

Pasta machine This can be used for rolling out clay to different thicknesses and is useful when precision and evenness are required, especially when producing several sheets of the same thickness. It can also be used for mixing colors. Buy one just for use with polymer clay and do not wash it between different colors, just wipe it clean with a cloth.

Dust mask Always wear a dust mask when sanding or drilling baked polymer or when using bronze powders.

Aluminum foil Layers of foil can be used to create bulk when making up shapes.

Waxed paper Tape a sheet of waxed paper to your work surface to ensure a smooth area. Also useful as a non-stick surface for baking clay.

Punches Metal- and leather-working punches are good for indenting and texturing clay surfaces.

Dentistry tools These precision tools are excellent for modeling. Ask your dentist for old ones or buy them from modeling shops.

Cookie cutter Good for patterns or cutting zigzag edges.

Dividers Useful for marking circular shapes to be cut out.

Toothpicks Good for reinforcing structure, especially joints.

Straws These can be used for making holes big enough for ribbon to pass through or for hanging over a nail.

Kebab sticks Use these to hold beads during baking.

Scissors are an essential piece of equipment useful for cutting out cardboard or paper templates.

Cheese slicer This can be used for taking even slices from an oblong cane.

Soft dough cutters For cutting out a wide variety of shapes, dough cutters are useful, but you may have to trim the edges of plastic ones to make them sharp enough for a clean cut.

Airtight box Polymer clay has a shelf life of approximately 2 years but goes crumbly if exposed to heat and ultraviolet light. Wrap the clay in waxed paper before storing it in a box.

Craft knife and scalpel A craft knife is good for cutting out heavy-duty cardboard, while a scalpel is perhaps the most useful tool for working with polymer clay.

Plastic cutting mat To protect your work surface, always cut clay on a cutting mat. Scrub the mat thoroughly to remove all traces of clay after use, as residues seem to react with the mat material.

Tissue blade Designed for taking human tissue samples, these razor-sharp blades enable thin slices to be cut from clay and are especially useful in canework and detailed modeling.

Round-nosed jewelry pliers Use these when making polymer jewelry pieces.

Pliers are essential for bending wire used structurally in projects.

Wire cutters are for cutting wire.

Vinyl gloves Many people prefer to wear gloves to protect their hands. Others wear them so as not to leave fingerprints on the clay. Gloves should be changed with each change of color to avoid transferring residual polymer particles from one color to another.

Fine palette knife This is useful for lifting thinly rolled out polymer clay.

Paintbrushes are essential for applying bronze powders and paints.

Plate A plate is useful for mixing paint colors.

Steel ruler A steel ruler guarantees straight lines.

Rolling pin A vinyl or straight-sided glass roller is best for rolling out clay by hand, although marble is excellent during hot weather, especially if the clay is overworked.

Brayer Sometimes referred to as a small roller, this is a good implement for smoothing over clay and wrinkled paper, or for applying metal leaf.

Plexiglass rollers A homemade device consisting of a small sheet of plexiglass with a wooden block as a handle is excellent for rolling out logs and canes. Make two sizes, about 3 inches x 3 inches and 8 inches x 7 inches for rolling out different sized items.

Petit four and aspic cutters are handy for cutting out interesting shapes.
Clay extruder Difficult to use, but useful if you do a lot of polymer clay work, this device should be secured with a small vice. Clay must be soft or thinned before use.

Smoothing tools These rubber-tipped implements for smoothing areas smaller than your fingertips resemble paintbrushes.

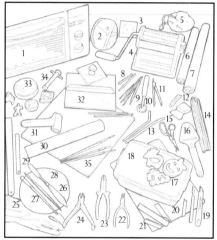

KEY

1 Oven
2 Mirror
3 Oven thermometer
4 Pasta machine
5 Dust mask
6 Aluminum foil
7 Waxed paper
8 Punches
9 Dentistry tools
10 Cookie cutter
11 Dividers
12 Toothpicks and cocktail sticks
13 Straws
14 Kebab sticks
15 Scissors
16 Cheese slicer
17 Soft dough cutters
18 Airtight sandwich box
19 Craft knife and scalpel
20 Plastic cutting mat
21 Tissue blade
22 Round-nosed jewelry pliers
23 Pliers
24 Wire cutters
25 Vinyl gloves
26 Fine palette knife
27 Paintbrushes
28 Plate
29 Steel ruler
30 Rolling pin
31 Brayer
32 Plexiglass rollers
33 Petit four and aspic cutters
34 Clay extruder
35 Smoothing tools

BASIC TECHNIQUES

POLYMER CLAY IS A WONDERFULLY VERSATILE MATERIAL, WHICH CAN BE SHAPED, MOLDED AND MODELED IN VARIOUS WAYS TO PRODUCE QUITE DIFFERENT EFFECTS. INSTRUCTIONS ARE GIVEN HERE FOR THE GENERAL TECHNIQUES WHICH HAVE BEEN APPLIED TO MANY OF THE PROJECTS IN THIS BOOK, SO DO READ THROUGH THIS SECTION CAREFULLY BEFORE EMBARKING ON A PROJECT. AS POLYMER CLAYS WILL PICK UP ANY DIRT AND DUST AROUND, IT IS IMPORTANT TO MAKE SURE YOUR HANDS ARE SCRUPULOUSLY CLEAN. YOU WILL ALSO NEED TO WASH YOUR HANDS WHEN CHANGING FROM ONE COLOR TO ANOTHER AS ANY RESIDUES WILL DISCOLOR THE NEXT PIECE OF CLAY YOU KNEAD.

PREPARING POLYMER CLAY

Polymer clays need to be manipulated or kneaded before they can be worked, the degree varying according to the brand. As clays are responsive to temperature, the warmth of your hands contributes to the conditioning process, and there is a world of difference between working with clay on a cold winter's day and on a hot summer's day. Some people go so far as to carry the clay in their pockets, or even bras, before working it.

To get your clay to its optimal working consistency, work small amounts, about an eighth of a block at a time, in your hands. Roll it between your palms to form a sausage, fold it over and roll again, then repeat the whole process until the clay is soft and pliable. Try to avoid trapping air bubbles in the clay. A pasta-making machine can be pressed into service to help the softening process.

MIXING COLORS

Although there are several commercially available colors, the choice becomes unlimited when you mix colors yourself. You can experiment by using small amounts to tailor colors to your needs. When mixing dark and light colors, add tiny bits of the darker clay to the lighter color as the darker one can easily overpower the lighter one.

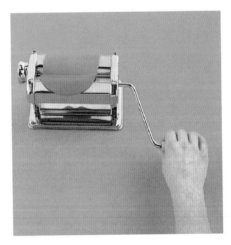

Mixing with a Pasta-making Machine

A pasta-making machine is excellent for mixing colors. Feed two differently colored sheets through the machine together, feeding them from opposite sides. As the sheets go through the machine they will become fused, and any air bubbles will be squeezed out.

Mixing by Hand

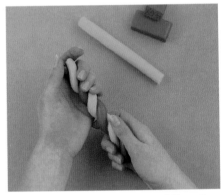

1 Twist together two or more differently colored sausages. This attractive effect is called candy cane.

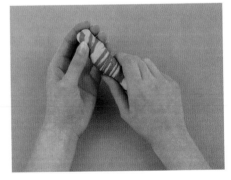

2 Roll the cane into a smooth log, then twist, stretch and double over, excluding any air bubbles, to achieve a marbled pattern. This is another stage that can be used as it is. To blend the colors completely, continue to work the clay as described.

Rolling Out

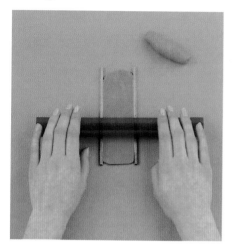

Roll the clay out on a smooth, clean surface, using a marble or acrylic rolling pin. A marble surface is excellent in a hot environment or if the clay is very soft, but not advisable in cold conditions. To ensure an even thickness, roll the clay between two pieces of metal, wood or plastic. Alternatively, pass it through a pasta-making machine, which is useful for producing several sheets of uniform thickness. If the clay is sticky, dust it with a thin film of flour or talcum powder.

PATTERNING

Patterned blocks can be used for various decorative effects. For instance, the slices of the striped block are used in the Eye-catching Cutlery project and to represent fabric in the Magnetic Theater project, while slices of the checkerboard design are used to make the hat of one of the players in the Magnetic Theater project. Slices can be cut off the block with a tissue blade or, if the block is long, with a cheese slicer.

Striped Block

1 Roll out several sheets of differently colored clay, trim them to the same dimensions, and stack them on top of each other, smoothing each layer to exclude air bubbles. Make the last layer a different color from the first. Trim the edges to neaten, if necessary.

2 When you have stacked a few layers, cut the block in half horizontally and stack. Roll with gentle pressure using a brayer.

Checkerboard Block

1 Make up a striped block. Using a tissue blade, cut off a slice the same thickness as the stripes. Stand the slice up alongside the block, staggering the colors, and cut another slice. Press this against the first slice and repeat the process to create a checkerboard block. Placing a mirror behind the block will help ensure that you slice the clay evenly.

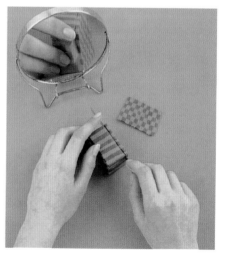

2 Press each side of the block evenly against a flat surface to consolidate it and trim if necessary.

Polka Dots

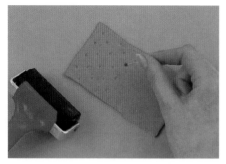

1 Press the head of a glass-headed pin into a rolled-out sheet of clay to make a regular pattern of indentations.

2 Roll out a thin sausage or cane in a contrasting color and slice off small disks using a scalpel. Roll these into balls and press each one into an indent.

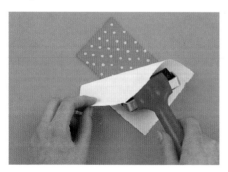

3 Place a smooth piece of paper over the clay sheet and roll using a brayer or pass through a pasta-making machine to smooth the surface.

Jelly roll

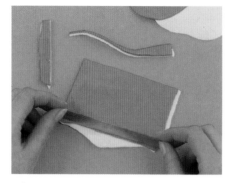

1 To make a jelly roll, roll out two or three differently colored sheets and stack them. Trim to neaten the edges into a rectangle.

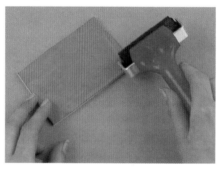

2 Roll over one of the shorter edges with a brayer to taper it.

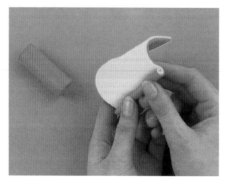

3 Starting at the flattened end, roll up the layers tightly and evenly. Gently roll the cane to smooth over the seams. Trim each end flat.

MAKING BEADS

Beads can be made in all sorts of shapes and sizes. A simple round bead is made by rolling a small ball of clay between the palms of your hands. Flat round ones are made by cutting thick disks from a log. More complicated beads can be made following the technique described in the Composite Beads project. Making the hole through the middle can be tricky, as the bead has to be held firmly enough to take pressure without distorting the shape. For this reason, many people prefer to drill the hole after the clay has been baked. Make the hole large enough to take whatever the bead is to be threaded on.

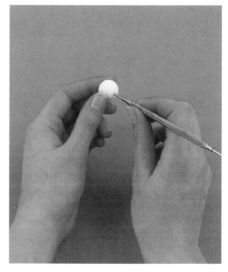

1 Make a hole through an unbaked bead using a tapered point such as a thin modeling tool or darning needle, with a drilling action. When the point emerges from the other side, remove the tool and push it through from the other side to neaten the hole. After the bead has been baked, you may need to sand down around the hole gently, using sandpaper, so that there are no jagged edges which could snag or catch on hair or clothing. ▶

2 Beads need to be supported during baking to keep their shapes from distorting. String the beads on wooden skewers or wire, depending on the size of their holes, and suspend them across a baking tray; make a wire support if you make beads regularly. If you are drilling the holes after baking, place them in the folds of corrugated cardboard to bake them.

CANE WORK

Deriving from ancient glassworking techniques, a cane is a log with a design running along its length, like a stick of rock. The designs can be simple or complex patterns or images. Thick slices cut from these canes can be made into beads or pendants. Thin slices can be used like a veneer to decorate beads or sheets of clay. Slices are best cut using a tissue blade. If necessary, chill the cane before slicing to avoid distorting the shape of the soft clay.

Canes can be reduced in diameter to make delicately small designs which may also be joined together to make complex designs such as millefiori beads.

The simple flower cane shown here is used in the Night Light and the Magnetic Theater projects. There is sufficient cane for both projects, plus enough left over for making into beads.

Simple Flower Cane

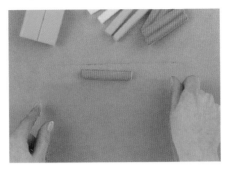

1 Roll one cane for the flower center (yellow), two canes of another color (green) and five canes from a third color (pink) for the petals. Make all the canes with a diameter of about ³⁄₄ inch and a length of 3 inches.

2 Roll out two thin sheets in different colors (coral and red) to cover the flower center, and a large thin sheet in a color to contrast with the petals (purple). Wrap the canes in these sheets, rolling each slightly to smooth the joints.

3 Using a tissue blade, cut the green canes lengthwise into quarters.

4 Roll out a thin sheet of an entirely different color (blue). Arrange the canes to form a flower, filling in the spaces between the petals with five of the quarter canes.

5 Wrap the bundle in the prepared sheet, rolling lightly to smooth the joint.

6 Using a small sheet of plexiglass, roll the cane to compact it. The ends will become concave. Trim these off.

Simple Picture Cane

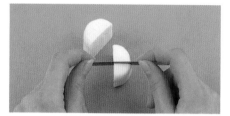

1 Roll a cane of white polymer clay about $1\frac{1}{2}$ inch in diameter and 3 inches long. Using a tissue blade, cut the cane in half lengthwise, then cut one of the halves into two to make two quarters.

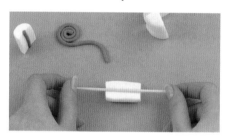

2 Roll one of the quarters into a round cane and cut it in half lengthwise. Press a groove down the middle of one flat side with a thin, round wooden or metal skewer and run a thin sausage of blue clay along it. Groove the other half and sandwich the two halves together to make the head and eye. Roll lightly to smooth the joints.

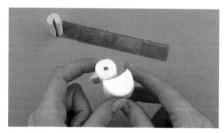

3 Curve the remaining half of the original white cane to form the duck's body. Place the head on the body. Cut a triangular wedge from a $\frac{1}{2}$ inch diameter yellow cane 3 inches long and press it firmly against the head for the bill.

4 Pack the gaps around the duck with wedges of pale blue cane, rolled to the same length, to make a circular shape. Wrap this with a thin sheet of pale blue to hold it together, and roll to consolidate it.

5 Surround the new cane with a sheet of dark blue, and roll again, smoothing the join. Trim off the concave ends.

Reducing Canes

Roll a cane under a small sheet of plexiglass to elongate it and reduce its diameter. Trim off the resultant concave ends as you work.

To make canes with different diameters with the same design running through them, stop rolling at each desired size and cut the cane in half. Continue rolling one half while reserving the other. Repeat until you have the sizes of cane you require.

Complex Canes

Gently squeeze several previously reduced picture or flower canes together and roll to produce a fascinatingly complex cane.

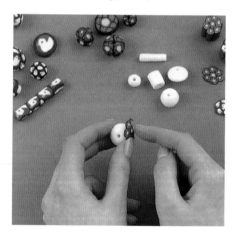

To make millefiori beads, cut thin slices from complex canes and press them onto the surface of clay beads. Previously baked beads give a better overall shape, but the millefiori slices may not adhere as well as on unbaked ones. Cover the bead completely and roll it between your palms.

METALLIC FINISHES

Polymer clays can be finished with metallic powders or metal leaf. Metal leaf may be gold, silver, copper or aluminum and is available in book form from art supply outlets. The sheets are very thin and easily marked by fingerprints so be careful when handling.

Metallic powders are brushed onto the surface of the clay. They go a long way, so use sparingly. For permanence, they should be varnished. As the particles of these powders are minute and spread everywhere, a fine dust mask should always be worn when using them.

Using Metal Leaf

1 Carefully lay a sheet of transfer leaf over a sheet of rolled-out polymer clay with the metal face down. As you lay it down, roll over it using a brayer to eliminate air bubbles. Rub all over the backing tissue paper before gently and slowly peeling it off. If any metal leaf clings to the tissue paper, replace it and rub over the area with your finger.

2 If you want a cracked finish, cover the surface of the applied metal leaf with a smooth piece of paper or tissue and roll over it using a brayer until the required amount of cracking is achieved. The cracking on silver and gold is finer than on copper or aluminum.

EMBOSSING AND TEXTURING

Being soft and pliable, polymer clay is easy to texture. It will take the impression of any pattern you press onto it, such as lace, a shell or a button. Alternatively, a pattern can be sculpted on using modeling tools or leather- and metal-workers' chasing and punching tools. Textured clay can be used to make molds for embossing other pieces of clay with a design.

1 Make a mold, such as the cup-shaped one shown here for making buttons, and transfer a relief design to it by pressing it into the clay. Bake the mold following the manufacturer's instructions, then use it to make positive images on other pieces of raw clay.

2 To highlight a textured piece before embossing, lightly brush the mold with metallic powder.

SPANGLY STARS

STARS ARE A PERENNIALLY POPULAR MOTIF, WELL SUITED TO LIGHTING. LOTS OF THEM CAN BE QUICKLY STAMPED OUT FROM A SHEET OF POLYMER CLAY TO WHICH GOLD LEAF HAS BEEN APPLIED. ALTERNATIVELY, PAINT THE STARS WITH GOLD PAINT AFTER THEY HAVE BEEN STAMPED OUT.

IF YOU MAKE A HOLE IN ONE POINT OF THE STARS, THEY CAN BE DANGLED FROM THE EDGE OF THE LAMP SHADE.

YOU COULD ALSO MAKE LOTS OF STARS FROM GLOW-IN-THE-DARK POLYMER CLAY AND HANG THEM FROM A CHILD'S BEDROOM CEILING.

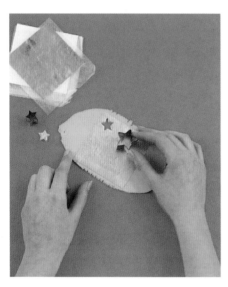

1 Apply gold leaf to rolled-out clay. Using small cookie or aspic cutters, stamp out the stars. Make some of the large ones hollow by stamping out their centers with a tiny cutter.

2 To make hanging holes, pierce through the center of the small stars and a point of the large ones using one of the jewelry head pins. If you wish, indent the centers of the small stars with a pen cap for decoration.

4 Attach the stars to the lampshade using double-sided tape or jewelry head pins pushed through the holes and the shade. Twist the wires behind the shade to hold the stars in position.

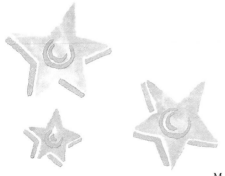

3 Lay the stars flat on a sheet of waxed paper and bake according to the manufacturer's instructions. When cool, apply varnish to protect the gold leaf.

MATERIALS AND EQUIPMENT YOU WILL NEED

SMALL BLOCK YELLOW POLYMER CLAY • DUTCH GOLD LEAF • STAR-SHAPED COOKIE OR ASPIC CUTTERS • JEWELRY HEAD PINS • LAMPSHADE • STRONG DOUBLED-SIDED TAPE • ROUND-NOSED JEWELRY PLIERS • VARNISH • PAINTBRUSH

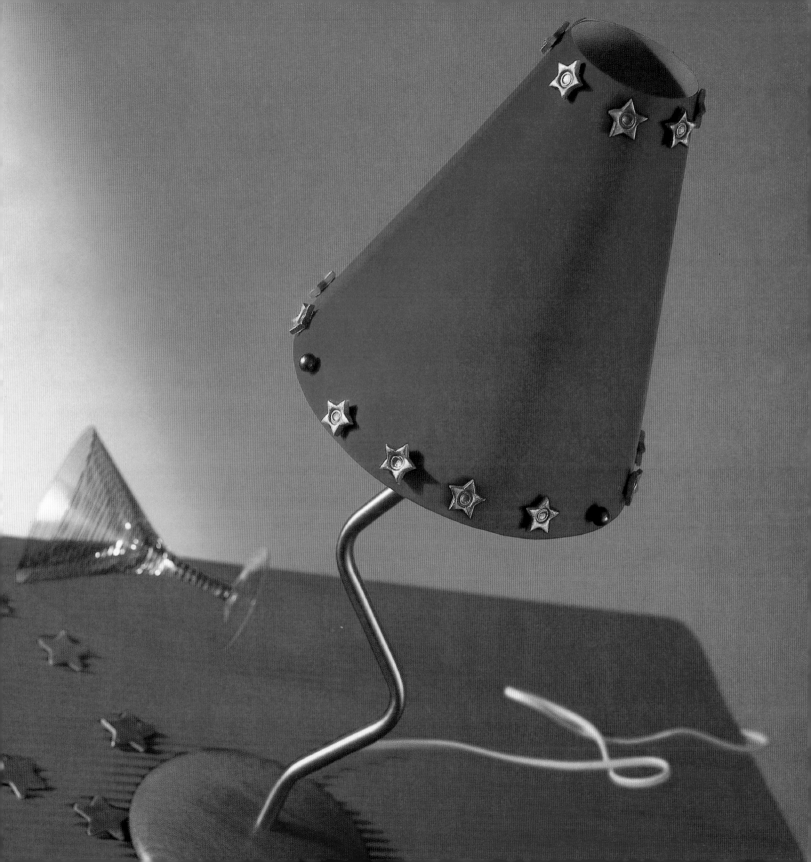

JAZZY TASSELS

Tassels are expensive to buy and are usually made in an old-fashioned style, but these black-striped, fluorescent versions, which make use of inexpensive silky tassels, are fresh and lively (for suppliers see back of the book). The polymer clay beads are modeled around a cork wrapped in aluminum foil which is removed after baking to create a hollow head through which the tassel end is threaded. Make pairs of tassels for tiebacks on curtains or single ones as light pulls.

1 Attach a marble on top of a cork or similarly shaped object using plasticine. Wrap a doubled strip of aluminum foil around the cork and secure with masking tape. Pinch the foil together at the top of the shape.

3 Snip off the excess clay at the top and smooth over to round the tassel top's shape. Push a sharp implement through the foil from the top to ensure the hole will be big enough for the tassel string. Bake for 5 minutes.

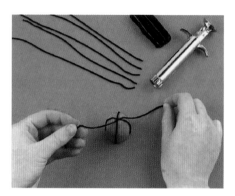

5 Roll or extrude thin threads of black clay. Drape over the top, tucking the ends inside at the bottom. Cut off the excess.

2 Roll out some modeling clay and cut a strip to wrap around the cork with enough to be pinched in at the top.

4 Pass a sharp implement through the hole at the top to push the cork out through the bottom of the tassel top. Roll out a thin sheet of fluorescent pink clay and wrap it around the tassel top. Cut off the excess and smooth over the joint.

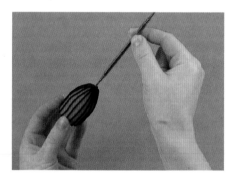

6 Press down where the threads cross over the top. Pierce through the hole once again. Return to the oven and bake for another 10 minutes. Thread the tassel through the top.

MATERIALS AND EQUIPMENT YOU WILL NEED

MARBLE • CORK OR SIMILAR SHAPE • PLASTICINE • ALUMINUM FOIL • SCISSORS • MASKING TAPE • $\frac{1}{8}$ BLOCK MODELING POLYMER CLAY • SHARP IMPLEMENT SUCH AS CROCHET HOOK • CRAFT KNIFE • $\frac{1}{2}$ BLOCK FLUORESCENT PINK POLYMER CLAY • SMALL AMOUNT BLACK POLYMER CLAY • EXTRUDER • TASSEL

BRIGHT BUTTONS

Finding just the right buttons can sometimes be tricky, especially if you want them for a garment of your own creation. With polymer clay you can design your own buttons and be as flamboyant as you like. At their simplest, polymer clay buttons can have two holes pricked through them for the thread. Alternatively, they can be glued onto button backs; the ones used here are intended to be covered with fabric, but polymer clay can be pressed onto them instead.

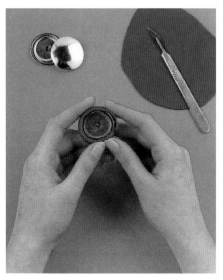

1 Snap together the two parts of each button back. Roll out colored clay to cover the front of the button and tuck the edges into the groove at the back.

2 Make a five-petalled flower template out of cardboard and cut one flower per button from white clay.

3 Place a flower on each clay-covered button, cover with a piece of paper and smooth over with your finger to make a good bond.

4 Make small balls of contrasting colors to the flowers, squash into disks and press firmly in place as flower centers. Smooth away any fingerprints.

Materials and Equipment You Will Need

Metal button backs • 1 block white polymer clay • Small amounts polymer clay: purple, turquoise, fluorescent green, yellow and pink • Cardboard • Scalpel • Smooth paper

SPOTTED EGG CUPS

COVERING METAL OBJECTS WITH POLYMER CLAY IS A SHORTCUT TO CREATING A SHAPE, LEAVING ONLY THE DECORATION TO BE APPLIED. THE METAL MUST NOT BE PREVIOUSLY PAINTED OR VARNISHED. HERE, STAINLESS STEEL EGG CUPS HAVE BEEN USED, BUT SALT AND PEPPER SHAKERS COULD ALSO BE TREATED (AFTER REMOVING THE PLASTIC STOPPERS), AS COULD TIN BOXES, WHISTLES OR CUTLERY. A THIN LAYER OF POLYMER CLAY APPLIED OVER A METAL BASE REQUIRES JUST 10 MINUTES BAKING TIME; LEAVE IT IN THE OVEN FOR A WHILE AFTER TURNING IT OFF, TO COOL DOWN.

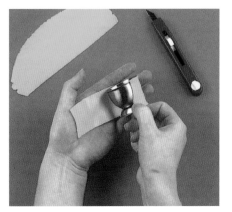

1 Roll out a thin sheet of yellow clay and cut out a strip to wrap around an egg cup.

3 Using the beaded head of a pin make small indentations in the clay in a regular pattern.

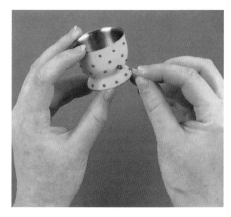

5 Use the beaded head of the pin to push the balls firmly in position, flattening them.

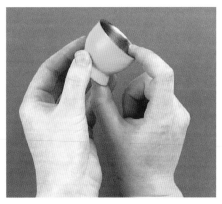

2 Smooth the clay to fit the contours of the egg cup and to join the ends together. Trim off any excess.

4 Roll a thin sausage of red clay. Cut into slices and roll each into a tiny ball. Pick each one up with the sharp end of the pin and place on an indentation.

6 Roll a slightly thicker red sausage to wrap around the rim, waist and bottom. Overlap the ends, trimming diagonally to fit, and smooth joints with fingertips or a smoothing tool. Bake the egg cups at a lower temperature and for a shorter time than recommended by the manufacturer.

MATERIALS AND EQUIPMENT YOU WILL NEED
1 BLOCK YELLOW POLYMER CLAY • 4 METAL EGG CUPS • GLASS-HEADED DRESSMAKER'S PIN • 1 BLOCK RED POLYMER CLAY •
CRAFT KNIFE • SMOOTHING TOOL

CHEERY CANDLE HOLDER

THE STAINED GLASS EFFECT OF THIS CANDLE HOLDER GIVES OUT A WARM GLOW WHILE PROTECTING THE FLAME. A VARIATION ON TRADITIONAL MILLEFIORI WORK, THIN SLICES OF FLOWER CANE ARE ROLLED OUT AND USED TO LAMINATE A GLASS TUMBLER. THE SAME TECHNIQUE CAN BE USED TO DECORATE GLASS JARS, PANES OF GLASS OR EVEN GOLDFISH BOWLS. WHEN POLYMER CLAY IS USED THIS THINLY, THE BAKING TIME SHOULD BE REDUCED BY HALF; IT IS POSSIBLE TO BAKE IT WITH A HAIRDRYER IF YOU CAN ASCERTAIN THE TEMPERATURE.

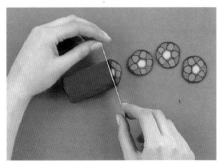

1 Cut five slices from the flower cane, all the same thickness (see Basic Techniques).

3 Run the brayer up and down the extra center cane to shape it into a triangular log. Cut off ten slices and roll them out thinly as described in step 2.

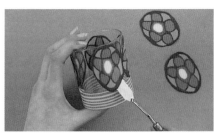

5 Wrap the striped slices around the bottom of the tumblers. Cut off any extra and smooth the joints. Using the palette knife, carefully transfer the flowers to the sides of the tumbler.

2 Place a piece of paper over one of the slices and roll the brayer over it in different directions to thin out the flower design with minimal distortion. Check regularly that the edges are not splitting. Roll the other slices.

4 Make a striped block and shave off two strips using the cheese slicer. Roll these between paper until they stretch about 1 inch in length.

6 Fill the gaps between the flowers with the triangular slices. Edge the top with a thin strip of blue clay. Place the tumbler on its side and roll firmly over a hard surface. Place in the oven before it heats up and bake, reducing the recommended cooking time by 5 minutes. Allow to cool completely before removing.

MATERIALS AND EQUIPMENT YOU WILL NEED

$2\frac{1}{2}$-INCH FLOWER CANE PLUS CENTER CANE (SEE BASIC TECHNIQUES) • CRAFT KNIFE • SMOOTH PAPER • BRAYER •
1 INCH X 4 INCHES STRIPED BLOCK OF POLYMER CLAY: FLUORESCENT YELLOW AND ORANGE (SEE BASIC TECHNIQUES) •
CHEESE SLICER • GLASS TUMBLER • PALETTE KNIFE • SMALL STRIP BLUE POLYMER CLAY

MINIATURE THEATER

THIS ENCHANTING THREE-DIMENSIONAL PICTURE SCONCE ENSHRINES THE MYTHICAL UNICORN IN A THEATRICAL SETTING. IT CAN BE HUNG ON A WALL BY A RIBBON OR PLACED ON A SHELF. THE FRAMEWORK IS MADE FROM COLLAGED AND PAINTED CARDBOARD, WHILE THE UNICORN ITSELF IS VERY SIMPLY MODELED OUT OF POLYMER CLAY. TO ENLARGE THE TEMPLATE FOR THIS AND OTHER PROJECTS, DRAW A GRID OF 1-INCH SQUARES AROUND THE TEMPLATE. DRAW A SEPARATE GRID OF LARGER SQUARES AND COPY THE TEMPLATE ONTO IT.

1 Draw the theater plan on thick cardboard and cut out, scoring along the dotted lines (see template at the back of the book). Make a small hole where shown for hanging.

3 Glue the wings to the front at all points of contact. Fold along all the score lines. Glue the top backdrop to the edges of the wings.

5 Shape the unicorn form. Pinch out the head, legs and tail shape, using a modeling tool for detail if you wish. Bake the unicorn following the manufacturer's instructions. When cool, smooth with wet-and-dry sandpaper if necessary.

2 Using gouache paint, paint the theater frame outside purple, the stage yellow, and the ceiling blue with yellow stars. When the paint is dry, paint the backdrop blue with yellow stars. Embellish further if you wish. Stick a photograph of a pair of velvet curtains to the front. When dry, varnish the front for protection.

4 Fold the sides in and glue along the edges and adhere to the back.

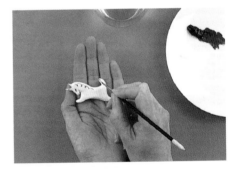

6 Paint the unicorn white. When this is dry, add detail in pale purple. Varnish and allow to dry. Apply glue to the feet and stand in position center stage, propping up if necessary with plasticine.

MATERIALS AND EQUIPMENT YOU WILL NEED

PENCIL • 1/8 INCH THICK CARDBOARD • STEEL RULER • SCALPEL • GOUACHE PAINT: PURPLE, YELLOW AND BLUE • PAINTBRUSHES • SCISSORS • FURNISHING CATALOG • SPRAY ADHESIVE • ACRYLIC VARNISH • STRONG GLUE • MODELING POLYMER CLAY • MODELING TOOL (OPTIONAL) • WET-AND-DRY SANDPAPER • ACRYLIC PAINT: WHITE AND PALE PURPLE • PLASTICINE (OPTIONAL)

ABSTRACT BARRETTE

HERE, SILVER LEAF IS APPLIED TO GLOW-IN-THE-DARK POLYMER CLAY WHICH IS THEN EMBOSSED WITH THE SPIRAL PATTERNS OF SOME OLD EARRINGS TO CREATE AN INTRIGUING EFFECT. IN THE DARK, A SUBTLE GLOW EMANATES FROM THE TINY CRACKS IN THE SILVER LEAF. YOU CAN USE ANY TYPE OF JEWELRY, AS THE PATTERN HAS A DISTINCT RELIEF. IF YOU DO NOT FEEL CONFIDENT ABOUT BUILDING UP YOUR OWN DESIGN, JUST REPEATEDLY PRESS A PIECE OF METAL OR PLASTIC JEWELRY INTO THE POLYMER CLAY.

1 Roll out some clay ¹/₈ inch thick. Draw the shape you want on cardboard, and cut it out. Place the cardboard on the clay and cut around it using a scalpel.

3 Create a regular pattern around the edge of the silver-leafed clay by pressing interestingly shaped jewelry, buttons, etc into it to leave indentations.

5 Wearing a dust mask, lightly brush the surface around the edge with bronze powder.

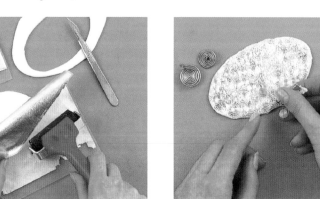

2 Apply silver leaf to the clay shape by passing a brayer over it (see Basic Techniques).

4 Fill in the central area with a random pattern applied in the same way as in step 3 but using different shapes if you wish.

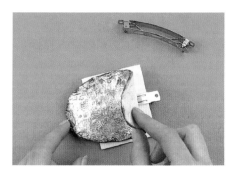

6 Slip a small piece of thin cardboard through the full width of the barrette then place the decorated clay shape on top. The clay will mold itself to the curved shape of the barrette but the cardboard will prevent it from sagging too much. Bake in this position, following the manufacturer's instructions. When cool, varnish the surface and glue the back onto the barrette.

MATERIALS AND EQUIPMENT YOU WILL NEED

¹/₂ BLOCK GLOW-IN-THE-DARK POLYMER CLAY • PENCIL • THIN CARDBOARD • SCISSORS • SCALPEL • SILVER LEAF • BRAYER • OLD JEWELRY OR BUTTONS • DUST MASK • DARK BLUE BRONZE POWER • BARRETTE • VARNISH • STRONG GLUE

TIGER DOOR PLAQUE

I MPISH TIGERS ARE USED HERE FOR A CHILD'S DOOR PLAQUE BUT YOU CAN MAKE ANY DESIGN YOU WANT WITH ANY MESSAGE. ATTACH THE PLAQUE USING HEAVY-DUTY SELF-ADHESIVE TABS. FOR OUTDOOR USE, COAT THE PLAQUE WITH AT LEAST TWO THICK COATS OF VARNISH AFTER MAKING A HANGING HOLE AT EACH CORNER. BE CAREFUL NOT TO TURN THE SCREWS TOO TIGHTLY WHEN ATTACHING IT.

THE INDIVIDUAL TIGER'S HEAD CAN BE USED TO MAKE BUTTONS. MAKE TWO HOLES WHERE THE NOSTRILS ARE FOR THE THREAD BEFORE BAKING.

1 Roll out a rectangle of white clay, about 5 inches x 3 inches x $\frac{1}{4}$ inch, to form the base plate. Make 12 strips 3 inches long and $\frac{1}{8}$ inch thick and lay them on the base.

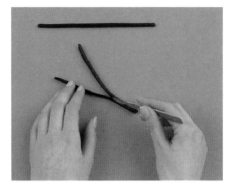

2 For the border, roll out two sausages from black clay, $\frac{1}{2}$ inch in diameter and a little longer than the base. Cut them in half lengthwise.

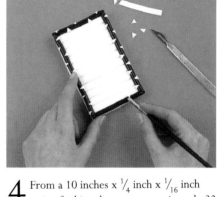

4 From a 10 inches x $\frac{1}{4}$ inch x $\frac{1}{16}$ inch strip of white clay, cut approximately 32 triangles. Arrange these at staggered intervals along the border.

3 Cut the black strips to fit the base, mitering the ends. Arrange them around the edge of the base, smoothing the joints.

5 To make the tigers' faces, roll three balls of white clay and flatten them to form disks about 1 inch in diameter and $\frac{3}{4}$ inch thick. Pinch out two ear shapes on each. Place a piece of paper over the shape, then smooth using the brayer. ▶

MATERIALS AND EQUIPMENT YOU WILL NEED
2 BLOCKS WHITE POLYMER CLAY • BRAYER • SCALPEL • $\frac{1}{2}$ BLOCK BLACK POLYMER CLAY • SMALL AMOUNT PINK POLYMER CLAY • SMOOTHING TOOL • SMOOTH PAPER

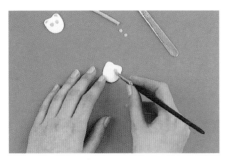

6 Roll a short $\frac{1}{8}$-inch-diameter cane from the pink clay and cut into nine slices $\frac{1}{16}$ inch thick. Roll each into a ball and flatten into $\frac{1}{4}$-inch-diameter disks. Place two disks on each face for the cheeks and smooth over. Cut the remaining three disks in half for the ear inserts and press in position.

7 Roll a thin thread of black clay and cut into six thin slices. Roll into balls and flatten for the eyes. Cut short lengths of black thread for the smiling mouths. Press into position.

8 Cut three triangles and three thin strips from the black clay to make the arrow-shaped noses. Press into position.

9 Cut 18 black triangles, long sides $\frac{1}{4}$ inch and short side $\frac{1}{8}$ inch. Place three triangles on each side of the faces. Cut nine thinner triangles and arrange them between the ears to make fringes.

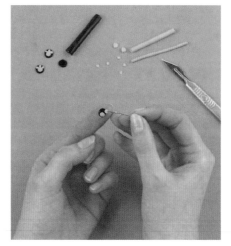

10 Roll a $\frac{1}{4}$-inch-diameter black cane. Roll two pink canes, one $\frac{1}{16}$ inch, the other $\frac{1}{8}$ inch in diameter. Cut four black disks, four from the thicker pink cane and 12 from the thinner pink cane. Roll the disks into balls and squash flat. Place one large and three small pink disks on each of the black disks to make the paws.

11 Roll a $\frac{1}{4}$-inch-diameter black cane, slice in half lengthwise and shape into letters. If more letters are required, make the cane narrower.

12 Arrange the tiger heads, paws and letters on the plaque and gently press them in place. Line a baking tray with waxed paper and bake following the manufacturer's instructions. Remove the paper immediately after baking.

MOBILE JUGGLERS

MOBILES CAN BE STRUCTURED IN AN INFINITE NUMBER OF WAYS, AND POLYMER CLAY IS LIGHT ENOUGH TO BE MADE UP INTO INTERESTING SHAPES TO SUSPEND FROM THEM. THEY ARE FUN TO MAKE AND WELL SUITED TO A CIRCUS THEME. HERE, FOUR JUGGLERS ARE MOD- ELED IN THE SAME BASIC SHAPE TO HANG IN FORMATION FROM A FRAME MADE OUT OF A BENT COAT HANGER. THESE JUGGLERS HAVE BEEN HAND PAINTED, BUT YOU COULD MAKE THEM USING BRIGHT POLYMER CLAY COLORS INSTEAD.

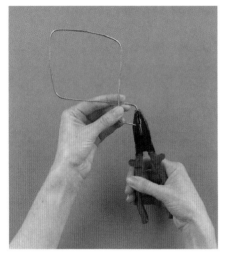

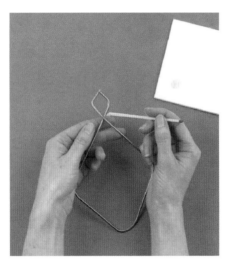

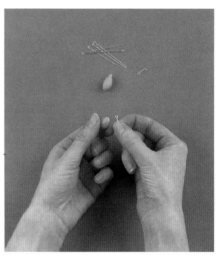

1 Using strong pliers or wire cutters, cut the hook and twisted section off a wire coat hanger and discard. Fashion half of the remaining wire into a double diamond shape as illustrated.

2 Spray the shaped wire with gold paint and glue the wires together to secure the point where they cross.

3 Mold four thumbnail-sized pieces of clay into egg shapes for the jugglers' heads. Trim an earring wire, form a hook in the end and embed this in one of heads. Repeat for the other heads. ▶

MATERIALS AND EQUIPMENT YOU WILL NEED

WIRE COAT HANGER • PLIERS OR WIRE CUTTERS • GOLD SPRAY PAINT • EPOXY RESIN GLUE • $\frac{1}{4}$ BLOCK MODELING POLYMER CLAY • EARRING WIRES WITH LOOPS • MODELING TOOLS • SCALPEL OR COOKIE CUTTERS • NEEDLE • WET-AND-DRY SANDPAPER (OPTIONAL) • ACRYLIC PAINT: PURPLE, RED AND YELLOW • PAINTBRUSH • VARNISH • NYLON FISHING LINE • SHELL-SHAPED JEWELRY CLASPS (OPTIONAL) • GOLD CORD OR RIBBON FOR HANGING

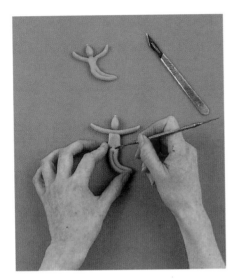

4 Roll a small sausage of clay for the arms and legs, and mold a rounded oblong for the torso. Assemble the parts, shaping the doubled legs into a curve. Using a modeling tool, smooth over the joints.

5 Roll out some clay and cut out four stars, two a little larger than the others, thick enough to be pierced by a needle. Either cut around a template using a scalpel or use cookie cutters. Roll five marble-sized beads. Pierce through all the pieces then bake them with the 4 jugglers' figures, following the manufacturer's instructions.

6 If necessary, smooth any rough edges using wet-and-dry sandpaper.

7 Paint a purple, red and yellow harlequin pattern onto the figures. Paint the beads red with a yellow pattern. Spray the stars gold. Varnish all these when the paint is dry.

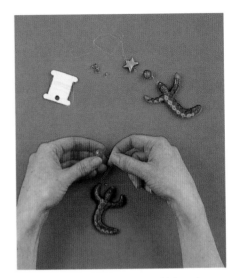

8 Loop a double thickness of fishing line through the ring on a juggler's head, and thread on a bead and a star. Use jewelry clasps to keep these in position, or knot the line, and glue them in place. Repeat for the other jugglers but do not thread a star for the fourth juggler.

9 Tie the jugglers to the wire shape, with the starless juggler tied to the top corner. Hang the remaining bead inside the small diamond. Dab glue on the knots to prevent the fishing line from slipping. Tie a length of gold cord or ribbon to the top for hanging. Glue the large stars on either side, sandwiching the wire in between.

POLY MERMAID

THIS DELIGHTFUL MERMAID WOULD ENJOY BASKING AMONG A COLLECTION OF SHELLS ON A SANDY SHELF IN A STEAMY BATHROOM. HER TAIL IS MADE OF STUFFED FABRIC AND IS DECORATED WITH ROWS OF BEADS AND SEQUINS. THE MODELING INVOLVED FOR HER TORSO, HEAD AND ARMS IS VERY SIMPLE, AND TRANSLUCENT CLAY IS USED TO GIVE HER A LOVELY WATERY HUE. THE MERMAID'S GOLDEN TRESSES ARE INGENIOUSLY MADE FROM AN UNRAVELLED PIECE OF CORD, WHICH IS GLUED ONTO HER HEAD.

1 Roll about a quarter of the clay into a ball and form into the mermaid's head. Draw out the neck to one side, rounding it off into a wider knob. Pinch out the nose and use a needle to make nostrils. Pierce a hole through the side of the neck, halfway down.

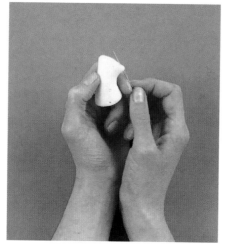

2 For the mermaid's midriff, roll a thick, stumpy log. Roll the middle between your index fingers to shape the waist. Make concave recesses in each end with your thumbs. Pierce holes at the front and back of the top and bottom.

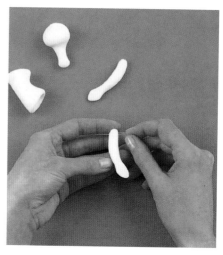

3 Fashion two stylized arms and hands and pierce the top of each with a needle. Bake all the body parts following the manufacturer's instructions. ▶

MATERIALS AND EQUIPMENT YOU WILL NEED
1 BLOCK TRANSLUCENT POLYMER CLAY • NEEDLE AND THREAD • ACRYLIC PAINT: BLUE, RED AND YELLOW • FINE PAINTBRUSH •
VARNISH • CARDBOARD • PENCIL • SCISSORS • 2 DIFFERENT FABRICS • WADDING • PIPE CLEANER • BEADS • SEQUINS •
GOLD CORD • GLUE

4 Wash the mermaid's face with soap and water to remove any surface grease. Using a fine paintbrush, paint on the features. Allow to dry.

5 Suspend each body part from a thread and dip it into varnish. Hang the pieces up until they are dry.

6 Make a template for the tail shape and cut out the fabric. Cut a bodice from different fabric. With wrong sides together, sew the seams then turn right side out. Gather in the top of the tail fin and sew to the tail. Pad the bodice with wadding and stitch across the top, leaving a gap for the neck.

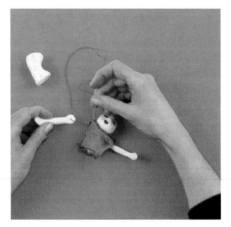

7 Insert the mermaid's neck and stitch the bodice to the neck. Attach the arms by sewing through the previously made holes to the bodice. Stitch the bodice to the top of the midriff, sewing through the previously made holes.

8 Push a pipe cleaner down inside the tail and stuff with wadding. Decorate the tail by sewing on rows of beads and sequins. Stitch the tail to the mermaid's midriff, sewing through the previously made holes.

9 Untangle a piece of cord and brush it out to make it look like hair. Glue the hair to the mermaid's head.

MIRROR WITH LIZARDS

DECORATED MIRROR FRAMES ARE VERY FASHIONABLE, AND THIS ONE IS EASY AND FUN TO MAKE. THE COLORFUL, BRIGHT-EYED LIZARDS WOULD BE IDEAL DECORATION FOR A CHILD'S BEDROOM, OR THEY WOULD ADD A WITTY NOTE TO YOUR BATHROOM WALL.

A CHEAP MIRROR WITH A PLASTIC FRAME WAS USED HERE. THE FRAME WAS BROKEN OFF WITH PLIERS AND REPLACED WITH POLYMER CLAY. THE REPEATING MOTIF IS A GOOD, RHYTHMIC WAY OF FILLING THE SHAPE, BUT A SINGLE LIZARD WOULD ALSO BE VERY EFFECTIVE.

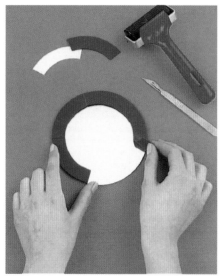

1 Roll out the light turquoise clay to about 3/16 inch thick. Cut five curved strips (see the template at the back of the book) and place carefully around the edge of the mirror.

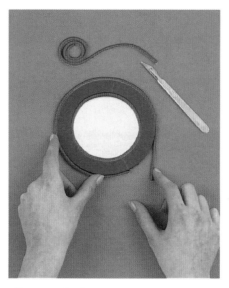

2 From the fluorescent mixed pink and magenta clay, roll out two long sausages, one slightly thicker than the other. Use the thinner sausage to edge the inner ring of the border, and the thicker sausage to edge the outer ring.

3 From the dark turquoise clay, fashion 20 lizard legs. Roll short sausages, flatten one end and bend for the knee and foot joints.

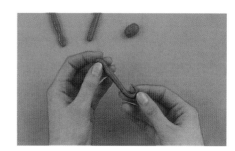

4 For each body, roll a tapered sausage from a medium-sized piece of dark turquoise clay. Create a neck in the thicker end by rolling between your two index fingers, and flatten out the head shape. Make four more lizard bodies. ▶

MATERIALS AND EQUIPMENT YOU WILL NEED

1 BLOCK LIGHT TURQUOISE POLYMER CLAY • BRAYER • SCALPEL • ROUND MIRROR, 5 1/4 INCH DIAMETER • 1/2 BLOCK FLUORESCENT MIXED PINK AND MAGENTA POLYMER CLAY (2:1) • 3 BLOCKS DARK TURQUOISE POLYMER CLAY • SMALL AMOUNT POLYMER CLAY: GRAY, BLACK AND WHITE • SMOOTHING TOOL • D-RING • EPOXY RESIN GLUE

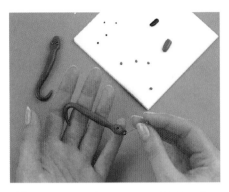

5 Roll tiny beads from gray, black and white clay for the eyes. Position the gray first and flatten, then add the black and finally the white on top.

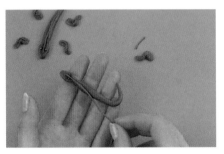

6 Roll thin strands of light turquoise clay to make a stripe for each lizard's back and its legs.

7 Make a thin tapering sausage from the pink clay and slice thinly to make subtly graded disks. Make approximately 18 per lizard. Roll the disks into balls, flatten and apply to either side of the back stripe.

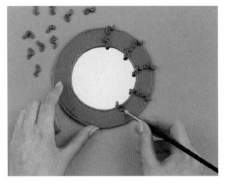

8 Position the legs at equal intervals on the mirror frame so that all the front legs cover up the joints. Press them into position using a smoothing tool.

9 Place the lizards' bodies on top of the legs, carefully but firmly enough to ensure that they join properly. Bake for three-quarters of the manufacturer's recommended baking time.

10 Form another, thicker pink sausage and flatten it into a flat circle using the brayer. Press it in position around the back of the mirror edge, making sure that it adheres well.

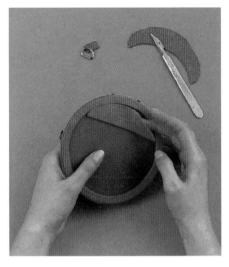

11 Roll out a thin sheet of pink clay and trim a semi-circular shape to fit within the back frame. Bake for the remainder of the recommended cooking time.

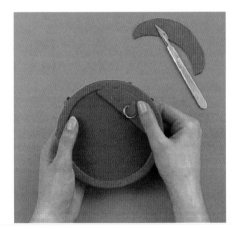

12 To position the D-ring for hanging, loop a thin strip of clay through the ring and make an indentation on the semi-circular shape but do not attach it yet. Remove the strip and the semi-circle and bake separately on a flat surface. When cool, glue the shape to the back of the mirror then glue the tab, making sure the D-ring can still move freely.

CHRISTMAS DECORATIONS

CHRISTMAS COOKIE CUTTERS ARE IDEAL FOR MAKING YOUR OWN DECORATIONS — NOTHING COULD BE EASIER! DECORATE THE SHAPES WITH A MODELING TOOL AND BRUSH ON YOUR OWN PATTERN WITH BRONZE POWDER. GLUE ON SMALL RHINESTONES FOR EXTRA SPARKLE.

INSTRUCTIONS ARE GIVEN HERE FOR MAKING ONE DECORATION, BUT YOU WILL PROBABLY WANT TO MAKE SEVERAL, USING DIFFERENT CHRISTMAS SHAPES. AS WELL AS HANGING THEM ON THE CHRISTMAS TREE, YOU CAN SUSPEND THEM FROM A DOOR KNOCKER OR CHRISTMAS WREATH.

1 Roll out the clay and press out a shape using a cookie cutter.

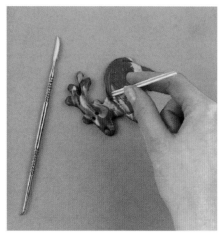

3 Using a plastic straw, make a hole in the center top for hanging.

5 Apply a protective coat of varnish.

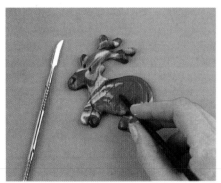

2 Draw on markings with a modeling tool and make small indentations for the rhinestones with the blunt end of a paintbrush.

4 Brush on differently colored bronze powders and blend together. Bake following the manufacturer's instructions.

6 Glue rhinestones in the indentations, using a toothpick. Thread a hanging ribbon through the hole.

MATERIALS AND EQUIPMENT YOU WILL NEED

POLYMER CLAY • ROLLER • CHRISTMAS.COOKIE CUTTERS • MODELING TOOL • PAINTBRUSH • PLASTIC STRAW • BRONZE POWDER: VARIOUS COLORS • VARNISH • RHINESTONES • GLUE • TOOTHPICK • RIBBON

MAGNETIC THEATER

BRING THE THRILL OF THE THEATER TO YOUR OWN HOME WITH THIS WONDERFUL MINIATURE THEATER. YOUR CHILDREN'S IMAGINATIONS WILL SUPPLY THE REST. THE SCENERY BACKDROP IS REVERSIBLE TO DEPICT NIGHT OR DAY. OTHER CHARACTERS CAN BE CREATED TO SUIT YOUR OWN STORY, BUT ALWAYS USE THE SAME BASIC BODY SHAPE AS IT IS THE MOST STABLE. THE MAGNETS MUST ALL BE INSERTED THE CORRECT WAY IN THE BASE OF THE FIGURES TO ATTRACT THEM TO THEIR OPPOSITE POLES IN THE CONTROL STICKS.

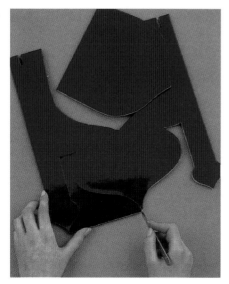

1 Spray-mount the mirror board onto the polyboard. When dry, draw the shape of the theater (see the template at the back of the book), then cut out using a scalpel and, for the sides, a steel ruler.

2 Glue star sequins to decorate the domes. Back strips of gold foil with double-sided tape. Draw, then cut out a sawtooth pattern. Stick the foil around the arch, towers and parapets.

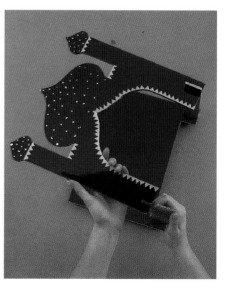

3 For the reversible backdrop, spray-mount each side of a piece of polyboard with different colored cardboard. Cut it out, along with the two side struts. Glue gold foil to the strut ends. Assemble the theater, using the hard cardboard for the base. ▶

MATERIALS AND EQUIPMENT YOU WILL NEED
SPRAY ADHESIVE • SHEET BLUE MIRROR BOARD • SHEET POLYBOARD • PENCIL • SCALPEL • STEEL RULER • GLUE •
STAR SEQUINS, MIXED COLORS • GOLD FOIL • DOUBLE-SIDED TAPE • SHEET ROYAL BLUE CARDBOARD • SHEET FLUORESCENT GREEN
CARDBOARD • SHEET VERY HARD CARDBOARD (FOR THE FLOOR) • SHEET DARK GREEN CARDBOARD • SCISSORS

FOR THE PLAYERS
1 BLOCK POLYMER CLAY: LIGHT AND DARK BROWN • PLEXIGLASS • SMALL MAGNETS • COCKTAIL STICKS •
SMALL GREEN BEADS • GLASS-HEADED DRESSMAKER'S PIN • SPOTTED POLYMER CLAY (SEE BASIC TECHNIQUES) OR FABRIC SCRAP •
MODELING TOOL • POLYMER CLAY: FLUORESCENT ORANGE, FLUORESCENT GREEN AND BLACK • WIRE • PEN •
BRONZE POWDERS • LEAF-SHAPED COOKIE CUTTER •
$3/4$-INCH FLOWER CANES (SEE BASIC TECHNIQUES) OR PLAIN CANES • PENCILS • GLUE

4 To make the figures, mix light and dark brown clay to the required shade. For the head, roll a small bead. For the body, roll a $1\frac{1}{4}$ inches diameter log about $\frac{3}{4}$ inch long. Press down more firmly on one side as you roll it, to make a cone shape.

6 Trim a toothpick just long enough to connect the head and body. Push it into the top of the cone, pointed end up. Add features to the head, using small glass beads for eyes and a tiny clay bead for the nose. Push the head onto the body.

8 For the arms, roll two thin sausages of brown clay. Flatten one end for hands and mark fingers using a modeling tool.

5 Press a magnet into the base of the cone, letting it stick out just a bit so that it will glide easily.

7 Wrap the body in a sheet of spotted clay, other patterned clay or, after it has been baked, in fabric. Make a fluorescent green beret from a flat pancake of clay with a fluorescent orange pompom.

9 Attach the arms to the sides of the body, pressing firmly. Make the other two figures the same way, but make their shapes different. ▶

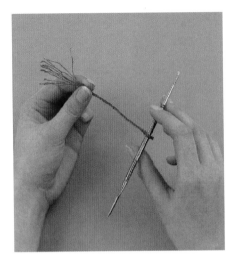

10 To make the black cat, roll a bead for the head and a dumpy cone for the body, as in step 4. Pinch the bead into a cat's head and attach to the body with a trimmed cocktail stick.

12 To make the tree, cut eight pieces of wire about 8 inches long. Double these over and insert a pen or similar object in the loop. Holding the wires about $2\frac{1}{2}$ inches from the cut ends, twist the wire to form the trunk's core.

14 Make bronze-coated variegated leaves (see Burnished Bronze Necklace project) and slot onto the twigs. Brush on purple bronze powder and bake following the manufacturer's instructions.

11 Roll a thin, tapered sausage for the cat's tail. Use two small beads for the eyes and attach two triangular-shaped ears to the head. Attach the tail. Bake all the figures following the manufacturer's instructions.

13 Roll scrap clay into a cone, then push the wire core through the pointed end to embed it in the clay. Roll again to finish the cone's shape. Divide the wires into groups of three and twist each group into branches, splaying out the ends as twigs. Trim into shape.

15 To make the magnetic operating sticks for the players, bore a hole in the sides of the flower cane disks to fit the sharpened end of a pencil. This will distort the disk, so trim it even. Bake the disks, then glue the pencils in position and glue a magnet onto each flower center.

BURNISHED BRONZE NECKLACE

POLYMER CLAY SIMPLIFIES THE CRAFT OF JEWELRY-MAKING BECAUSE STONES, WHICH WOULD NORMALLY HAVE TO BE SET IN METAL, CAN SIMPLY BE PUSHED INTO THE CLAY. METAL LEAF AND POWDERS READILY ADHERE TO THE SLIGHTLY STICKY SURFACE OF UNBAKED CLAY TO GIVE IT A LUSTROUS RICHNESS. THIS NECKLACE IS MADE USING A BROAD RANGE OF COLORS, BUT YOU COULD JUST USE ONE IF YOU PREFER. GLASS BEADS ARE USED TO COMPLETE THE NECKLACE, BUT YOU COULD MAKE YOUR OWN BEADS AND COAT THEM WITH METALLIC POWDER.

1 Roll out a piece of black clay, about $3/16$ inch thick, and cut it in half. Dust lines of the bronze powders onto the surface of one piece.

3 Roll the remaining piece of clay slightly thinner and cut it into five or six squares, each 2 inches. Place a length of jewelry wire centrally on each square and place a stone on top, slightly off center, to allow room for the leaves. Cut $1/8$-inch-wide strips from the remaining bronzed clay and wrap these around the stones, cutting off the excess.

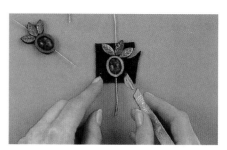

5 Press the leaves and stone gently but firmly enough to meld them together and to hold the stone securely in place. Cut out around the shape using a scalpel and smooth along the joint at the sides to eliminate it. Bake following the manufacturer's instructions.

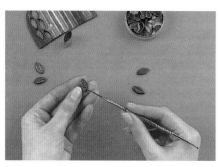

2 Mark vertical lines between the colors, then cut out leaf shapes so that the lines form the central veins. Press in other veining with a modeling tool.

4 Arrange three leaves to one side of the stone. The wire should consistently project from the same side of the middle leaf on each square, to allow the necklace to hang in a tight-fitting curve.

6 Carefully varnish the bronzed areas and allow to dry. Using jewelry pliers, make loops with the wire ends, trimming off excess wire. Hook the pieces together and close up the hooks. Attach the beads at each end of the necklace in the same way and wire on a clasp.

MATERIALS AND EQUIPMENT YOU WILL NEED

1 BLOCK BLACK POLYMER CLAY • DUST MASK • BRONZE POWDERS: VARIOUS COLORS • PAINTBRUSH • LEAF COOKIE CUTTER • MODELING TOOL • JEWELRY WIRE • SCALPEL • WIRE CUTTERS • GLASS CABOCHON STONES • VARNISH • JEWELRY PLIERS • BRONZED POLYMER BEADS OR GLASS BEADS • CLASP

EYE-CATCHING CUTLERY

EVEN THE MOST BORING CUTLERY CAN BE GIVEN A NEW LEASE ON LIFE WITH A SET OF POLYMER CLAY HANDLES. HERE, A BASIC SHAPE IS USED, BUT MORE ADVENTUROUS SHAPES CAN BE SCULPTED.

BECAUSE CUTLERY HAS TO STAND UP TO A LOT OF WEAR AND TEAR, USE THE STRONGEST MAKE OF POLYMER CLAY FOR THE INNER LAYER. FOR THE OUTSIDE, ANY OF THE BRANDS WILL DO. ONCE BAKED, POLYMER CLAY IS WATERPROOF, BUT IT IS A GOOD IDEA TO TREAT THE CUTLERY AS IF IT WERE BONE-HANDLED.

1 For each piece of cutlery, roll out the clay to about ⅛ inch thick and cut into strips. Place two strips around the handle, pressing along the sides to seal.

3 Roll out a sheet of polka dot clay to the width you require and wrap around the middle of the handle, making the joint at the back.

5 Cut two strips of the second striped clay and wrap around the handle to cover the joints. Join at the back, cutting the ends diagonally to make a good fit.

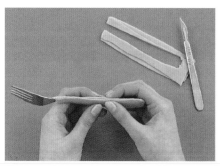

2 Trim around the handle shape and smooth over the joint. Cover all the cutlery handles in this way, then bake following the manufacturer's instructions.

4 Cut four thin slices of striped clay and wrap these around the top and bottom of the handle. Make the joint at the side and try to make it on the darker color. Smooth over the joint.

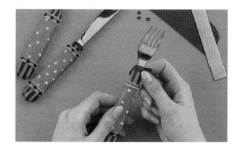

6 Using a pin head, make three indentations on each strip, on the front of the handle. Roll three tiny blue balls and press on. Smooth the clay at the top, then wrap with a thin blue strip. Bake, following the manufacturer's instructions. Apply a double coat of varnish when cool.

MATERIALS AND EQUIPMENT YOU WILL NEED
2 BLOCKS MODELING POLYMER CLAY • BRAYER • CUTLERY • SCALPEL • POLKA DOT POLYMER CLAY (SEE BASIC TECHNIQUES) • SMOOTHING TOOL • STRIPED POLYMER CLAY (SEE BASIC TECHNIQUES), IN 2 COLORS • TISSUE BLADE • GLASS-HEADED DRESSMAKER'S PIN • DARK BLUE POLYMER CLAY • MATTE VARNISH

EGYPTIAN BANGLE

IT IS HARD TO BELIEVE THAT THIS EXOTIC-LOOKING PIECE OF JEWELRY IS MADE FROM A SHORT LENGTH OF PLASTIC PIPE SURROUNDED BY POLYMER CLAY. MUCH OF THE TRANSFORMATION IS BROUGHT ABOUT BY THE APPLIED GOLD LEAF AND EMBEDDED STONES. LINE THE INSIDE OF THE PIPE WITH A THIN LAYER OF THE STRETCHED GOLD CLAY.

TO CUT THE PIPE TO LENGTH, MARK A LINE AROUND AND SAW THROUGH IT WITH A HACKSAW. ALTERNATIVELY, ASK THE STORE TO CUT IT TO THE SIZE YOU REQUIRE.

1 Roll out a strip of clay large enough to cover the section of plastic pipe. Apply the gold leaf and crackle the surface using a brayer (see Basic Techniques).

2 Cut the clay exactly to size and wrap it carefully around the pipe, making sure there are no air bubbles.

3 Smooth the joint, taking care not to rub off any gold leaf. ▶

MATERIALS AND EQUIPMENT YOU WILL NEED
PLASTIC DRAINPIPE • 1 BLOCK BLACK POLYMER CLAY • DUTCH GOLD LEAF • BRAYER • SMOOTHING TOOL • MODELING TOOLS •
GEMSTONES • EPOXY RESIN GLUE • ACRYLIC PAINT: SEVERAL COLORS • FINE PAINTBRUSH

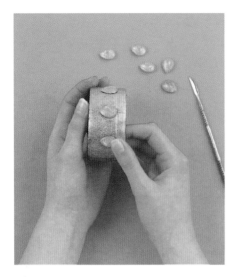

4 Using a modeling tool, faintly mark a line around the circumference ¹/₂ inch from one edge. Measure the circumference, divide the figure by the number of stones you wish to use and mark spacings along the line. Press the stones into the clay.

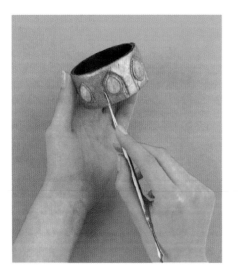

5 Draw a line around each stone, then press an arch around it.

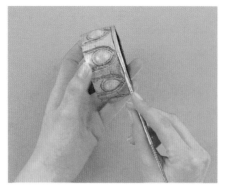

6 Draw a line around the bangle along the top of the arches.

7 Etch a narrow arch between adjacent arches all around the bangle. This will form the central petal of the stylized Egyptian flower.

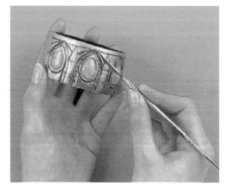

8 Draw a pointed petal on either side of the central ones, then add smaller ones in between.

9 Carefully remove the stones and bake the bangle following the manufacturer's instructions. When cool, glue the stones back in place.

10 Paint the flowers and background sections in colors of your choice.

COMPOSITE BEADS

ONCE YOU HAVE MASTERED THE ART OF MILLEFIORI (SEE BASIC TECHNIQUES), YOU WILL BE ABLE TO USE IT IN A NUMBER OF EXCITING WAYS.

HERE, SLICES FROM A PICTURE CANE, COMBINED WITH A FLOWER CANE AND A COLORFUL JELLY ROLL, ARE APPLIED TO PARTIALLY BAKED POLYMER CLAY BEADS. WHEN FULLY BAKED, THESE WONDERFULLY DECORATIVE BEADS CAN BE STRUNG TOGETHER TO MAKE NECKLACES. REMEMBER TO MAKE HOLES IN THE UNBAKED BEADS.

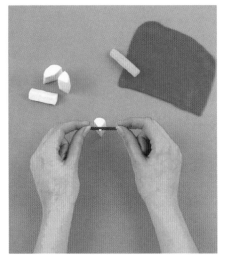

1 Roll a 1¼-inch-diameter log of white clay. Cut it into five wedges from the center and slice off the sharp angle of each wedge. Roll out a 2½-inch yellow cane and a flat sheet of green clay.

2 Arrange the white triangular wedges, separated by ⅛-inch slivers of green, around the central yellow cane to form a flower. Roll the cane, using a sheet of plexiglass to smooth.

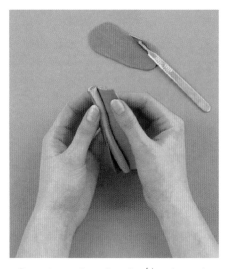

3 Make a jelly roll with 1½ inches x 4 inches strips of yellow and fluorescent orange clay (see Basic Techniques). Wrap the roll in a thin sheet of pale blue clay, about 1/16 inch thick. ▶

MATERIALS AND EQUIPMENT YOU WILL NEED

1 BLOCK WHITE POLYMER CLAY • SCALPEL • TISSUE BLADE • ¼ BLOCK YELLOW POLYMER CLAY • 1 BLOCK GREEN POLYMER CLAY • PLEXIGLASS • ½ BLOCK FLUORESCENT ORANGE POLYMER CLAY • ¼ BLOCK PALE BLUE POLYMER CLAY • 2½ INCHES OF 1 INCH DIAMETER PICTURE CANE (SEE BASIC TECHNIQUES) • 8 INCH FLOWER CANE • ½ BLOCK CORAL POLYMER CLAY • VARIOUS-SHAPED POLYMER CLAY BEADS (SEE BASIC TECHNIQUES)

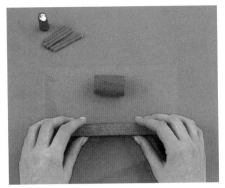

4 Reduce the picture cane to $\frac{1}{2}$ inch in diameter and the flower cane and jelly roll to about $\frac{1}{4}$ inch (see Basic Techniques). Reserve the trimmings for making beads. Cut the jelly roll into 3-inch lengths. Cut a 3-inch length from the duck cane and set the surplus aside.

5 Cut the flower cane into four lengths of 3 inches. Arrange them in a cross pattern around the picture cane, interspersed with 4 jelly roll canes.

6 Roll the assembled canes carefully between your hands to meld them together, then wrap in a $\frac{1}{8}$-inch-thick sheet of green clay.

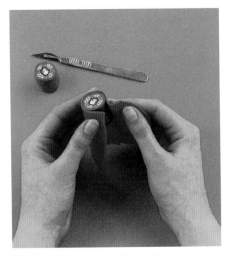

7 Cut the cane in half using a tissue blade; rock the blade while you cut to avoid distorting the picture. Wrap one of the halves in a $\frac{1}{8}$-inch-thick sheet of coral clay, cut off the surplus and roll under plexiglass to smooth the sides.

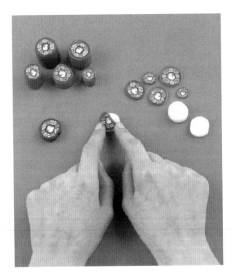

8 Make up several compilation canes, then reduce them further to different sizes. Shave off thin slices to cover the surface of previously prepared disk beads and roll them smooth. It is a good idea to make the canes and the beads compatible.

9 Use some of the surplus picture and flower cane to make borders or sides for the beads. Press them on firmly so they will adhere and smooth over.

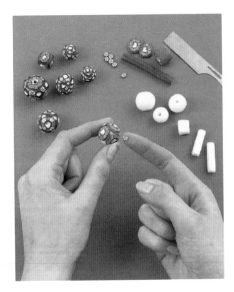

10 Cover previously prepared round beads, filling any triangular shaped gaps with slices of the surplus small flower or picture cane. If you cover any bead holes pierce through again after you have rolled the surface smooth. Bake all the beads following the manufacturer's instructions.

GLOW-IN-THE-DARK CLOCK

BECAUSE IT IS MADE WITH GLOW-IN-THE-DARK POLYMER CLAY, YOU WILL BE ABLE TO READ THE TIME FROM THIS AMUSING CLOCK IN THE DARK. THE FLOWER AND EGG MOTIFS ARE DETACHABLE, ALLOWING FOR OTHER ORNAMENTS, SUCH AS A CANDLE FOR A BIRTHDAY CELEBRATION (AS LONG AS THE CANDLE DOES NOT BURN RIGHT DOWN TO THE CLAY), TO BE ATTACHED TO THE CLOCK IN THEIR PLACE.

THE CLOCK MECHANISM IS INEXPENSIVE TO BUY (SEE PAGE 95 FOR SUPPLIERS) AND IS EASILY ASSEMBLED.

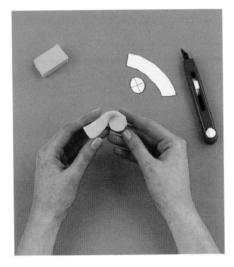

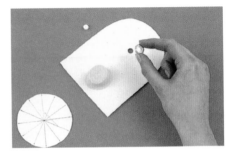

1 Roll out the glow-in-the-dark clay and trim to a 4-inch x 5-inch rectangle $^3/_{16}$ inch thick. Cut a circular template, place at one end and cut around it to shape the top. Squeezing an empty plastic film canister, stamp out an oval near the bottom.

2 Make templates for a slightly curved strip and for the oval cut out in step 1. Roll out a small quantity of yellow clay and cut out these shapes. Wrap the strip around the oval to form a tapered cup.

3 Fix the cup over the hole in the clock face and smooth over the joint. Mark the hour positions on the circular template and position it on the back plate. Prick through the center to mark the clock face. Using a narrow tube, stamp out a hole large enough to take the clock spindle.

4 Roll and cut out two strips of glow-in-the-dark clay $1^1/_4$ inches wide by $^3/_{16}$ inch thick. Make one $12^1/_4$ inches and the other 4 inches in length. Using a very narrow tube, stamp out a small hole at the mid-point of the longer strip. ▶

MATERIALS AND EQUIPMENT YOU WILL NEED

$2^3/_4$ BLOCKS GLOW-IN-THE-DARK POLYMER CLAY • CRAFT KNIFE OR SCALPEL • METAL RULER • THIN CARDBOARD • PENCIL • FILM CANISTER • $^1/_4$ BLOCKS POLYMER CLAY: YELLOW, LIGHT BLUE, DARK BLUE, LIGHT AND DARK GREEN • SMOOTHING TOOL • DRESSMAKER'S PIN • NARROW TUBES • JEWELRY WIRE • ALUMINUM FOIL • CROSSHEAD SCREW • BALLPOINT PEN • JEWELRY HEAD PINS • EPOXY RESIN GLUE • WIRE CUTTERS • CLOCK MECHANISM

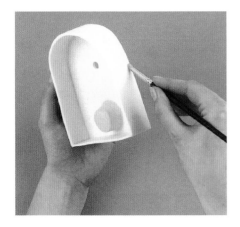

5 Assemble the strips to make the sides of the clock face, smoothing over the joints. Fix the sides to the back of the clock face and smooth over the joints.

6 Roll a marble-sized piece of light blue clay into an egg shape. Crumble some dark blue clay and roll the egg in it to speckle the surface.

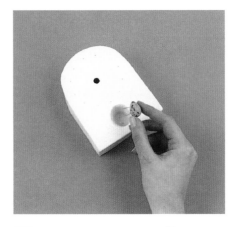

7 Push two short wires, about $\frac{5}{8}$ inch, into the egg. They should project sufficiently to push into the recess to hold the egg in place. Remove the egg and bake it following the manufacturer's instructions.

8 Cut a glow-in-the-dark clay rectangle to cover the bottom section of the back of the clock face. Fill up the cavity with scrunched-up aluminum foil. Bake the clock face following the clay manufacturer's instructions.

9 Twist together thin strips of yellow and light and dark green clay to create a marbled sausage.

10 Cut the sausage into one long and four short pieces. Assemble the pieces to make a central stem with four branches. Taper one end of the stem.

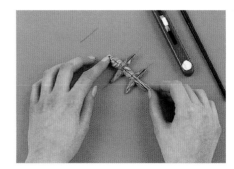

11 Make incisions along the branches and stem, and insert wires long enough to protrude from the ends of the branches and the non-tapered end of the stem. Close up the slits and smooth over. ▶

12 Roll out a small piece of yellow clay and form a three-petaled flower. Roll out a small piece of green clay and shape four leaves. Press patterns on the flower and leaves using the tip of a screw and a pen.

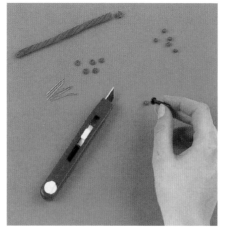

14 Twist together thin strips of light and dark blue clay and slice off 12 disks. Roll these into balls and flatten. Stamp each with the end of a screw and make a hole in the middle. Bake the disks following the manufacturer's instructions.

13 Push the flower and leaves onto the wires of the stem and branches and bake following the manufacturer's instructions. When assembled, the tapered stem slots into the hole at the top of the clock.

15 Push a jewelry head pin through each disk, dab a spot of glue on the back and push the pin into the clock face at an hour marking. When the glue has dried, snip off the excess wire at the back. Hold the clock movement at the back of the clock face. Push the spindle through the hole from the front and screw together.

PICTURE FRAME

THE RECIPE FOR THIS PROJECT WILL MAKE A BATCH OF EIGHT TO TEN PICTURE FRAMES. THE COLORS ARE BUILT UP IN BLOCKS OF CLAY, FROM WHICH YOU TAKE SLICES FOR EACH FRAME. TO MAKE A SINGLE FRAME, CUT OUT ALL THE BASIC SHAPES FROM $\frac{1}{16}$-INCH-THICK SHEETS OF GREEN POLYMER CLAY AND CUT OUT ALL THE DECORATION FROM BLUE AND BLACK SHEETS OF CLAY. LAY THEM ON TOP OF ONE ANOTHER AND ROLL OVER THEM TO ENSURE THEY ADHERE. MAKE THE HOLES AND EMBROIDER AS DESCRIBED.

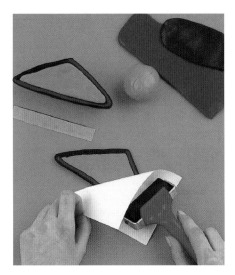

1 Thoroughly mix and blend the green and turquoise clays. Mold a block into a triangular wedge. Cover with a thin skin of black clay. Then cover two sides with a thick blue layer and one side with black. Surround the whole with a thin layer of black. Using the tissue blade, take off a thin $\frac{1}{8}$-inch slice across the wedge (see Basic Techniques). Place a sheet of smooth paper over this and roll the slice smooth. This will be the roof.

2 Make an oblong block in green, about $6\frac{1}{2}$ inches x 1 inch x $1\frac{1}{4}$ inches. Surround with a thin skin of black clay. Place a thick blue strip along the bottom. Cover the top two-thirds of the length with black and the remainder with blue and finally a thin layer of black. Make two smaller oblongs, about $2\frac{1}{2}$ inches x $\frac{3}{4}$ inch x $1\frac{1}{4}$ inches, one of black, the other of green. Slice both in half, then cut diagonally to make triangles.

3 Place a green triangle centrally on top of the oblong block. Add one on each side. Cut the remaining one in half and place at each end. Encircle the entire structure with a thin strip of black clay. Cover one side and halfway along the ridges with a thick blue layer. Cover the other side and the remaining ridges with a thick black layer. Then continue with a thin black layer over the blue right down the opposite side. ▶

MATERIALS AND EQUIPMENT YOU WILL NEED

1 BLOCK GREEN POLYMER CLAY • 1 BLOCK TURQUOISE POLYMER CLAY • LARGE BLOCK BLACK POLYMER CLAY • 2 BLOCKS BLUE POLYMER CLAY • SMOOTH PAPER • BRAYER • TISSUE BLADE • SCALPEL • NEEDLE • EMBROIDERY THREAD: BLUE AND YELLOW • CORRUGATED OR THICK CARDBOARD • KNITTING NEEDLE • JEWELRY HEAD PIN • JEWELRY PLIERS

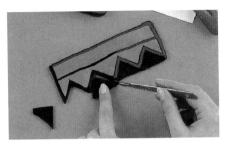

4 Invert the black triangles between the green ones and compress the whole assembly, without disorting any of it, to pack all the elements together. Using the tissue blade, take off a thin $\frac{1}{8}$-inch slice. Place a sheet of smooth paper over this and roll smooth. Cut out the black triangle, leaving a black edging. This will be the base.

5 Make up another block, like the base block in step 2, but wider, about $6\frac{1}{2}$ inches x $1\frac{1}{2}$ inches x $1\frac{1}{4}$ inches. Using the tissue blade, take off two thin $\frac{1}{8}$-inch slices the length of the oblong. Place a sheet of smooth paper over each and roll them smooth. These will be the sides.

6 Decorate the roof and sides. Make an oval cane of blue wrapped in black and cut three slices for the roof. Make long, thin blue and black sausages to make scroll patterns on the roof and sides. Cut tiny disks from the sausages to make spots.

7 Assemble the frame, securing the pieces with small pieces of black clay pressed across the joints at the back.

8 Referring to the finished illustration for guidance, use a needle to make stitching holes. Add more spots to balance the design if you like. Cover the back with a thin layer of black clay, cutting out the window. Place the frame, face up, on a sheet of waxed paper and bake following the manufacturer's instructions.

9 Stitch through the prepared holes with embroidery threads, referring to the finished illustration.

10 Roll out a $\frac{1}{8}$-inch-thick black rectangle, slightly larger than the window. Place it over a sheet of corrugated cardboard or other thick cardboard and press all around it to create a pocket. Pierce a hole near the top using a knitting needle and reinforce it with a ring of clay.

11 Make a small black-wrapped blue cane, press it into an egg shape and cut six slices. Sandwich a jewelry head pin between a pair of slices and kink the wire with pliers. Bake these with the pocket following the manufacturer's instructions.

12 Glue the pocket into position, pressing along the seams to ensure a good joint. The gap should be wide enough to slide in a piece of glass and a picture.

CACTUS CANDELABRA

THE CACTUS SHAPE MAKES A DRAMATIC, SCULPTURAL CANDELABRA, AND THE FLUORESCENT COLOR ENSURES IT WILL BE A FOCAL POINT IN ANY ROOM. A BASIC STRUCTURE MADE FROM WIRE AND ALUMINUM FOIL IS COVERED WITH A SKIN OF CLAY TO MAKE THE CANDELABRA AN ECO-NOMIC PROPOSITION. CHECK THAT THE DIMENSIONS OF THE CANDELABRA WILL FIT IN YOUR OVEN BEFORE STARTING WORK. IT WILL BAKE MORE QUICKLY AT THE TOP OF THE OVEN THAN AT THE BOTTOM, SO YOU MAY NEED TO ROTATE THE CANDELABRA DURING BAKING.

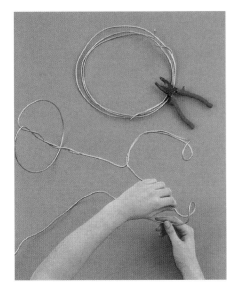

1 Work a long piece of wire into the basic structure of the candelabra. Make a circular base, bend the wire back to the center, then up to make the central stem. Form the three branches, looping the end of each in to make candle-holders. Twist the remaining end in.

2 Spread out five large sheets of foil, one on top of the other. Cut a piece of cardboard the size of a small plate and place it in the center of the foil. Stand the candelabra frame on the cardboard.

3 Fold up the foil, shaping it into a funnel around the wire frame.

4 Pour a pitcher of sand into the funnel to fill it out and also to weight the base of the candelabra.

5 Squeeze the foil together around the frame. Fold sheets of foil into thick strips and wrap these around the stem to make a bulbous shape. ▶

MATERIALS AND EQUIPMENT YOU WILL NEED

MALLEABLE WIRE, ABOUT 5 FEET • PLIERS • ALUMINUM FOIL • CARDBOARD • PLATE • SCISSORS • JUG • SAND • WIDE MASKING TAPE • 2 BLOCKS MODELING POLYMER CLAY • ROLLING PIN • SCALPEL • 2 BLOCKS FLUORESCENT GREEN POLYMER CLAY • POLYMER CLAY: FLUORESCENT PINK, ORANGE AND DARK GREEN • DRESSMAKER'S PIN • STRONG GLUE

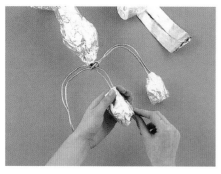

6 Roll the foil strips into cups and tuck them over the wire loops. Bind the cups in place to the required thickness using more folded foil.

7 Wrap masking tape around the structure to completely cover it.

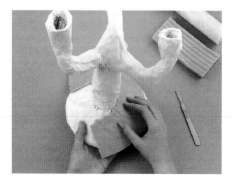

8 Roll the clay into broad strips, about $\frac{1}{8}$ inch thick, and cover the candelabra with them. Do not press too hard as this will spoil its smooth form. Smooth over the joints.

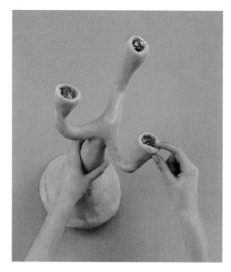

9 Tuck the ends of the clay over the candle-holder edges. Bake for 10 minutes.

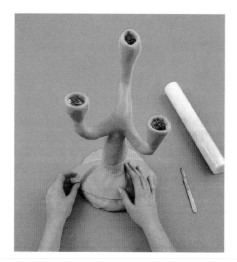

10 Roll out the fluorescent green clay into thin sheets and use it to completely cover the baked modeling clay, smoothing over the joints. Bake for another 10 minutes.

11 Roll one thick and one thin fluorescent green sausage, one thick fluorescent pink sausage and one thinner fluorescent orange sausage. Cut thin disks from all of these, make into balls, then flatten. Place pink dots on the larger green disks and orange dots on the smaller green disks. Pierce through both layers with a pin to help them hold together. Place the dots on a flat tray and bake following the manufacturer's instructions.

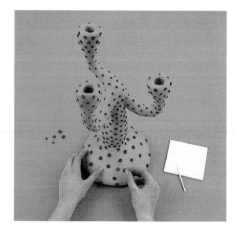

12 Glue the cooked dots to the candelabra to transform it into a cactus.

FUNKY FURNITURE

Jazz up a run-of-the-mill doll house with this funky set of minuscule fluorescent furniture. The clay is first made up into a striped block, a double-layered sandwich slab and a jelly roll. These are then cut into slices to make the furniture.

The quantities of clay quoted in the recipe are enough to make one polka-dot armchair, a table and a set of four dining chairs. Adjust the size of the furniture, if necessary to suit the dimensions of your own doll's lair.

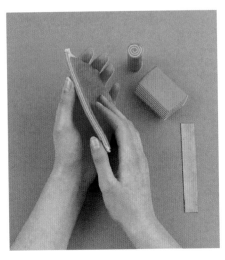

1 For the armchair, prepare the following from fluorescent orange and yellow clay: a $1\frac{1}{2}$-inch x $2\frac{1}{2}$-inch x 1-inch striped block; a double-layered sandwich slab, about $1\frac{1}{2}$ inches x $2\frac{3}{4}$ inches x $\frac{1}{4}$ inch; and a $2\frac{1}{2}$-inch length of $\frac{3}{4}$-inch-diameter jelly roll (see Basic Techniques).

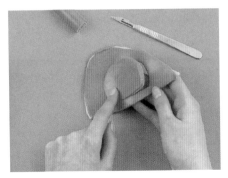

2 Cut out the armchair back from the double-layered slab using a scalpel. The base should be 2 inches wide. From top to base, it should be $2\frac{1}{2}$ inches and its broadest width should be $2\frac{3}{4}$ inches.

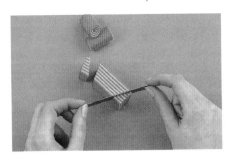

3 Cut three thin slices from the jelly roll and set aside. Cut the remainder in half. Holding a tissue blade at an angle, slice a wedge off each end of the striped block to make it trapezoidal.

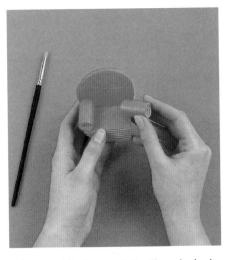

4 Assemble the armchair. Place the back on top of the trapezoid, longest length up, pressing firmly to secure it, then smooth over the joints. Place the halved jelly roll pieces on either side of the seat for arms and press the back into them. Then puff it out in the center by pressing with your fingers through the back. ▶

MATERIALS AND EQUIPMENT YOU WILL NEED

1 BLOCK FLUORESCENT ORANGE POLYMER CLAY • 1 BLOCK FLUORESCENT YELLOW POLYMER CLAY RULER • SCALPEL • TISSUE BLADE • SMOOTHING TOOL • GLASS-HEADED DRESSMAKER'S PIN • 1 BLOCK FLUORESCENT LIGHT TURQUOISE POLYMER CLAY • 1 BLOCK FLUORESCENT GREEN POLYMER CLAY • FLAT WOODEN TOOTHPICKS • PLEXIGLASS • COCKTAIL STICKS • WIRE-CUTTERS • EPOXY RESIN GLUE • PAIR OF DIVIDERS

5 Make a thin sausage of fluorescent yellow clay, slice it into small disks and roll into tiny balls. Apply the balls to the armchair to create a polka-dot pattern, using a glass-headed pin (see Basic Techniques).

6 Reinforce the back behind the armchair by running a length of flattened fluorescent orange sausage along the joint, then place the thin jelly roll slices along the ridge.

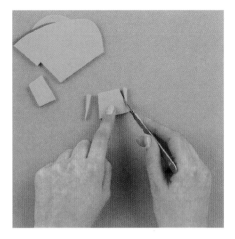

7 For the table and chairs, prepare a sandwich slab approximately $4\frac{3}{4}$ inches x 3 inches x $\frac{1}{4}$ inch (see Basic Techniques), using light turquoise and fluorescent green clay. For each chair, cut trapezoidal seats with the longest side $1\frac{1}{2}$ inches, its parallel 1 inch and the two sides $1\frac{1}{4}$ inches. Cut trapezoidal backs with the same length parallels but with sides of $\frac{3}{4}$ inch. Smooth around the edges.

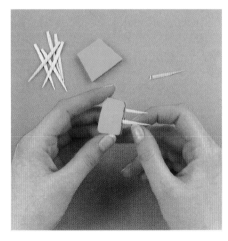

8 Push the wedge ends of three flat wooden toothpicks into the bottom edge of each chair back, leaving 1 inch protruding.

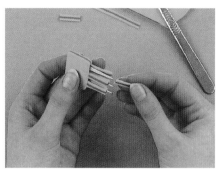

9 Cut six thin $\frac{3}{4}$-inch strips from the sandwich slab for each chair. Sandwich the toothpicks between these, leaving the points uncovered. Press between finger and thumb to join up at the sides.

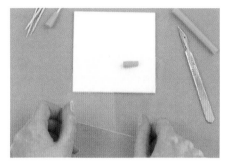

10 Roll a 3-inch-long, $\frac{1}{4}$-inch-diameter green clay log for each chair. Cut each one into four chair legs and taper the shape by rolling and pressing one end. Insert a cocktail stick into the narrower end of each leg. Bake the legs standing up, and the backs lying down, following the manufacturer's instructions.

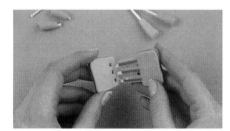

11 Press the baked backs into the unbaked seats to make holes. ▶

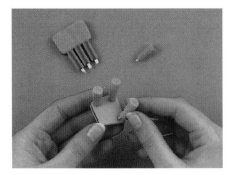

12 Trim the cocktail sticks in the legs, leaving just enough to embed in the seat. Press the legs into the undersides of the seats. Remove the legs and bake the seats.

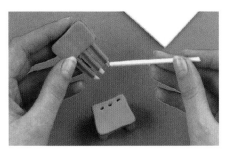

13 Assemble the chairs. Glue the legs in position. When the glue is dry, glue onto the chair backs. These will need supporting until the glue is dry.

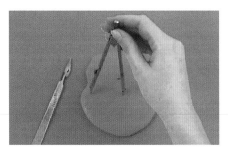

14 Make another sandwich slab measuring a minimum of $3\frac{1}{2}$ inches square. Using a pair of dividers, lightly mark a $3\frac{1}{2}$-inch circle. Mark a cross at the center and mark $\frac{3}{4}$ inch along each line from the centerpoint. Cut out the circle and smooth around the edge.

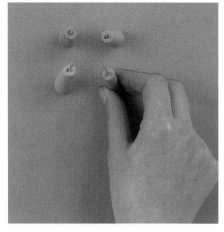

15 Roll a $5\frac{1}{2}$-inch-long, $\frac{5}{8}$-inch-diameter green clay log. Cut into 4 table legs. Taper them by rolling and pressing and insert cocktail sticks as described in step 10. Bake them standing up and leaning slightly inwards.

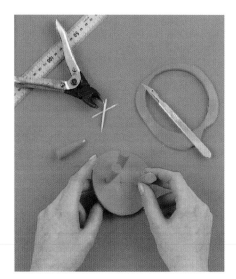

16 Trim the cocktail sticks, leaving just enough to embed in the tabletop. Press them into the table top to mark their positon, remove them and place the tabletop on a piece of waxed paper the right way up. Bake following the manufacturer's instructions. When cool, glue in the legs.

TINY TEA SET

THIS LILLIPUTIAN TEA SET WOULD MAKE A DELIGHTFUL PRESENT FOR ANY CHILD OR DOLL'S HOUSE ENTHUSIAST. POLYMER CLAY IS IDEALLY SUITED TO SMALL-SCALE WORKING AS ITS ELASTICITY ALLOWS FINE SHAPES AND DETAILS TO BE MODELED. THE COLORS REMAIN SEPARATE EVEN WHEN THE CLAY IS SQUASHED INTO A SMALL FORM. SPOTS ARE A CHEERFUL DECORATION AND EASY TO PAINT ONTO SUCH SMALL-SCALE ITEMS. YOU MAY PREFER TO USE A COLOR AND PATTERN TO MATCH AN EXISTING DOLL'S HOUSE DECOR.

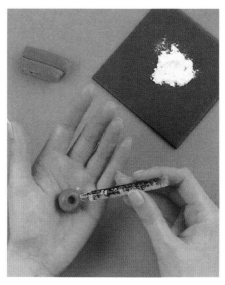

1 Roll a marble-sized piece of clay into a ball with your hands. Dip the end of a pen, or similar object, into the flour and push it into the ball with a screwing action to create a pot shape.

2 For the spout, roll a sausage shape and cut off a small amount. Roll this between your little fingers to taper the shape. Cut a small "V" out of one end.

3 Press the spout onto the pot and stroke the end into a curve.

4 Roll another, thinner, sausage and cut off enough for a handle. Fix the top of the handle by pressing the head of a pin on the underside, then loop the sausage over and fix the bottom. ▶

MATERIALS AND EQUIPMENT YOU WILL NEED

½ BLOCK POLYMER CLAY • 1 TEASPOON FLOUR OR TALCUM POWDER • PEN OR SIMILAR OBJECT • SCALPEL • GLASS-HEADED DRESSMAKER'S PIN • SMALL MARBLE • WASHERS: ¾ INCH AND ⅝ INCH • PALETTE KNIFE • SMALL CAN WHITE ENAMEL PAINT • PAINTBRUSH • VARNISH

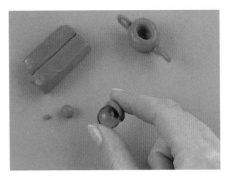

5 Roll three small balls, one pea-sized, one a little larger and one a little smaller. Squash the largest ball against a marble to shape it into a curved disk for the lid.

6 Press the smallest ball onto the lid to make a knob. Squash the pea-sized ball into a disk that will just fit inside the rim of the teapot, then press it in the center of the underside of the lid.

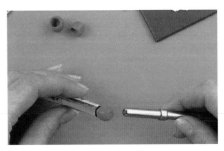

7 To make the tea cups, roll a pencil-thin sausage, and slice it into four lengths about 1/4 inch. Push the end of a pen, dipped in flour or talcum powder, into the end of each length to hollow it out. Before removing the pen, indent the other end of each cup so that they will stand up better.

8 Make each cup handle from a thin thread of clay, attaching it in the same way as for the teapot (see step 4).

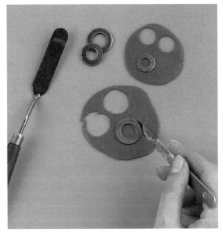

9 For the saucers and plates, use the washers as templates. Roll out a piece of clay about 1/8 inch thick and cut around each washer four times.

10 Hold the larger washer against each plate and push the end of a pen or similar object through the hole to make an impression for the inner circle.

11 Press the smaller washer against each saucer to make an indentation then curve it around the marble. Bake all the pieces in the oven following the manufacturer's instructions and allow to cool.

12 Decorate the tea set with tiny spots of white paint. Allow to dry, then varnish as required.

SHIMMERING EARRINGS

Since it is lighter than metal, polymer clay allows large, bold designs to be worn as earrings, especially when fitted as here with cushioned clips. The tiers of these glamorous earrings swing as the wearer moves, glittering as they catch the light.

For a less flamboyant version, make the earrings using only one of the tiers. Gold leaf scrolls, different-shaped gemstones and droplet beads all contribute to the effect, and the earrings are richly marked with decorative indentations and lines.

1 Cut 12 lengths of wire $\frac{3}{4}$ inches long and form a loop in one end of each. Cut two lengths of $1\frac{1}{4}$ inches and two of $2\frac{1}{2}$ inches and form loops at both ends of each. Cut a sheet of black clay into squares to make backing sheets: two $1\frac{1}{4}$-inch squares for the top tiers; two $1\frac{1}{2}$-inch x $1\frac{1}{4}$-inch for the central tiers; and two $\frac{5}{8}$-inch squares for the bottom tiers.

2 Lay three short wires along the bottom of each middle-sized backing sheet and press them in with the brayer. Lay a long wire down the center of each large backing sheet with a short, single-hooked wire on either side and press in. Lay the remaining short, single-hooped wires one on each of the small backing sheets and press in.

3 Press an oval stone onto each of the middle-sized backing sheets. Cut two strips, $\frac{1}{8}$ inch wide, from the gold-leafed clay and wrap securely around each stone, trimming off any excess. Add more strips to decorate.

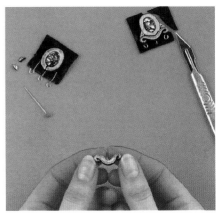

4 Cut two lengths, $1\frac{1}{4}$ inches, from the gold-leafed slab and pinch both ends to taper them. Shape into scrolls and press in position on the middle-sized backing sheets to cover the wires, pushing the wires in a bit more if necessary. Cut two small squares of gold-leafed clay, cut in half diagonally and place above the scrolls. Press decorative indentations and lines around the border with the head and shank of a pin. Trim off the excess backing sheet. ▶

MATERIALS AND EQUIPMENT YOU WILL NEED

JEWELER'S WIRE • WIRE CUTTERS • ROUND-NOSED JEWELRY PLIERS • $\frac{1}{4}$ BLOCK BLACK POLYMER CLAY • BRAYER • $\frac{1}{4}$ BLOCK BLACK POLYMER CLAY WITH GOLD LEAF APPLIED (SEE BASIC TECHNIQUES) • GEMSTONES: OVAL $\frac{1}{2}$ INCH LONG; RECTANGULAR $\frac{5}{8}$ INCH LONG; ROUND $\frac{1}{4}$ INCH DIAMETER • SCALPEL • DUTCH GOLD LEAF • DRESSMAKER'S PINS • PALETTE KNIFE • EYELET OR SIMILARLY SHAPED OBJECT • SMOOTHING TOOL • VARNISH • PAINTBRUSH • LARGE CLIP-ON EARRING BACKS • EPOXY RESIN GLUE • 10 DROPLET BEADS

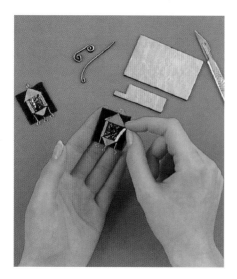

5 Press the square stones centrally onto the two large backing sheets. Cut a $\frac{5}{8}$-inch square and a $\frac{1}{2}$-inch square from the gold-leafed clay. Cut both of these in half diagonally to create four triangles. Press a larger triangle above each stone and a smaller one beneath. Cut four thin strips of gold-leafed clay to fit on each side of the stones.

6 Using a palette knife, press in all the pieces to secure a tight fit around the stones. Take care not to distort the shapes. Cut two thin strips $1\frac{3}{4}$ in long from the gold-leafed clay, curl them into scrolls and place one under each bottom triangle. Use an eyelet to stamp a circular marking on the top triangles.

7 Make six tiny beads, roll them in gold leaf, and use them to decorate the tops of the middle tiers. Trim off the excess backing sheet.

8 Place one of the remaining stones on each of the small backing squares. Cut two strips of gold-leafed clay $1\frac{1}{4}$ inches long and wrap them around the stones. Trim off the excess backing sheet.

9 Using a smoothing tool or your finger, go around the edges of each piece to make sure all the surfaces are melded together. Bake following the manufacturer's instructions and allow to cool.

10 Varnish all the gold leaf surfaces and allow to dry. Glue the clip-on earring backs to the backs of the first tier.

11 Join the tiers together, using jewelry pliers to close up the hooks.

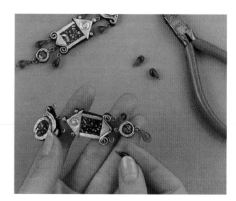

12 Hang droplet beads from the free hooks, closing up the hooks. The bottom droplets can be slightly bigger than the others.

STARBURST HAND MIRROR

"MIRROR, MIRROR ON THE WALL, WHO'S THE FAIREST OF THEM ALL?" ALTHOUGH THIS MIRROR IS NOT ATTACHED TO THE WALL, IT IS CERTAINLY REMINISCENT OF FAIRY TALES AND MYTHOLOGY. THE MAGICAL EFFECT IS ACHIEVED BY ENCASING THE MIRROR BETWEEN TWO LAYERS OF POLYMER CLAY WHICH HAVE BEEN COVERED WITH STRETCHED COPPER LEAF; COPPER LEAF CHANGES COLOR WHEN HEATED, ENHANCING ITS APPEARANCE. THE FRAME IS EMBELLISHED WITH GLASS GEMSTONES AND PAINTED. THE HANDLE IS REINFORCED WITH WIRE.

1 Roll out a 1/4-inch-thick sheet of polymer clay, about 1 1/2 inches larger all around than the mirror. Apply copper leaf and crackle the surface (see Basic Techniques). Press the mirror into the center of the clay to emb it firmly.

2 Cut two pieces of rectangular clay to form the handle. Press one into the edge of the mirror base. Prepare the second piece with crackled copper leaf as in step 1 and set it aside for use in step 8.

3 Prepare a thin strip of clay with copper leaf, rolled a little more thinly to give a finer crackle. Press it onto the clay base to frame the mirror.

4 Cut out three trapezoidal pieces of clay to form the three points of the cross. Apply copper leaf and crackle as in step 3, then press in place.

5 Using a modeling tool, press all around the inner and outer edges of the mirror frame to neaten them and to secure the mirror. Do the same around the cross points.

6 Place a small cabochon stone on the mirror frame opposite each cross point and the handle. Score the cross points outward to create a ray-like pattern. ▶

MATERIALS AND EQUIPMENT YOU WILL NEED

LARGE BLOCK BLACK POLYMER CLAY • COPPER LEAF • MIRROR • SCALPEL • MODELING TOOL • 4 SMALL BLUE GLASS CABOCHON STONES • WIRE • 3 LARGE GEMSTONES • ACRYLIC PAINT: MAUVE, CORAL, BLUE AND WHITE • PAINTBRUSH

7 Etch a double-tiered zigzag pattern radiating out from the mirror frame to produce a sunburst effect.

9 Carefully mold the zigzag sunburst pattern around the mirror frame to create a staggered ray effect, then cut off the excess clay using a scalpel.

11 Roll out a thin piece of clay and apply copper leaf to it. Cut it into three narrow strips and frame each gemstone with one. Press a pattern into the strips to secure the stones in position. Bake following the manufacturer's instructions.

8 Bend a piece of wire to form a hook at one end. Embed it along the length of the handle with the hook towards the mirror. Cover with the second part of the handle prepared in step 2, pressing the edges together.

10 Press the large gemstones along the handle and delineate around them using the modeling tool.

12 Highlight the details with differently colored paints: variegated mauve on the outer spikes; variegated coral on the inner spikes; variegated blue on the cross points and down the handle (see Ornamental Book Cover project, steps 10 and 11).

ORNAMENTAL BOOK COVER

A HANDSOME PLAQUE GLUED TO THE FRONT OF A CLOTHBOUND BOOK OR DIARY, OR TO THE LID OF A BOX, WILL MAKE IT INTO SOMETHING SPECIAL. THIS ONE IS MADE FROM A SILVER-LEAFED SLAB OF POLYMER CLAY WHICH HAS BEEN MOLDED AND PAINTED. SILVER AND GOLD LEAF LEND AN OPULENT FEEL, BUT A CHEAPER OPTION WOULD BE TO PAINT THE SLAB WITH METALLIC PAINT AFTER THE CLAY HAS BEEN BAKED. IF YOU WISH TO DEVISE YOUR OWN DESIGN, TRANSFER IT TO THE CLAY BY PRICKING THROUGH A PIECE OF PAPER WITH A PIN.

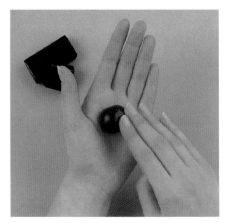

1 Cut off a quarter of the clay block and roll into a ball.

2 Squash the ball into a flat-bottomed dome.

3 Press a similarly sized, clean-edged circular object, such as a length of tubing, over the dome to give it a regular shape.

4 Dab silver leaf onto the dome to make irregular, map-like shapes, suggestive of a globe of the world.

5 Roll out a rough rectangle, about 3 inches x $4\frac{1}{2}$ inches x $\frac{1}{4}$ inch. Apply silver leaf to the surface and give it a fine crackle (see Basic Techniques). Lightly mark a cross to locate the center and press the dome shape into the clay. Cut out a true rectangle using a ruler and scalpel. ▶

MATERIALS AND EQUIPMENT YOU WILL NEED

LARGE BLOCK BLACK POLYMER CLAY • SCALPEL • CLEAN-EDGED CIRCULAR OBJECT • SILVER LEAF • ROLLING PIN •
METAL RULER • MODELING TOOLS • 4 BLUE GLASS CABOCHON STONES • ACRYLIC PAINT: TURQUOISE, PURPLE, BLUE, RED AND WHITE •
PAINTBRUSHES: FINE AND MEDIUM • VARNISH • EPOXY RESIN GLUE

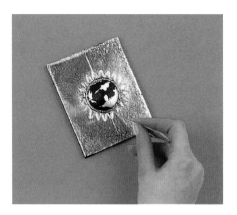

6 Delineate around the globe and score radial zigzag lines around it using a modeling tool or bent wire.

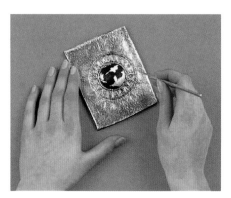

7 Encircle the zigzag pattern with two parallel circles and sculpt them in.

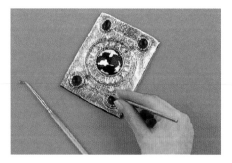

8 Place a blue cabochon stone in each corner. Encircle them with patterning as around the globe, connecting them at top and bottom with horizontal lines.

9 Roll out a thin sheet of clay, apply silver leaf to it, then cut it into strips. Cut each strip into a zigzag to make tiny triangles. Press these around each stone as decoration and to hold them firmly in place.

10 Paint on the base colors, leaving black edging around the "continents" on the globe. When dry, add white to all the colors except turquoise and paint thick stripes all over the base.

11 Add more white to the basic colors and paint on finer lines to create a variegated appearance.

12 Varnish the surface, taking care not to put varnish on the stones, and allow to dry. Glue onto a book or box.

TEMPLATES

MAGNETIC THEATER, PP54–57

LIZARD MIRROR, PP49–51

MINIATURE THEATER, PP36–37

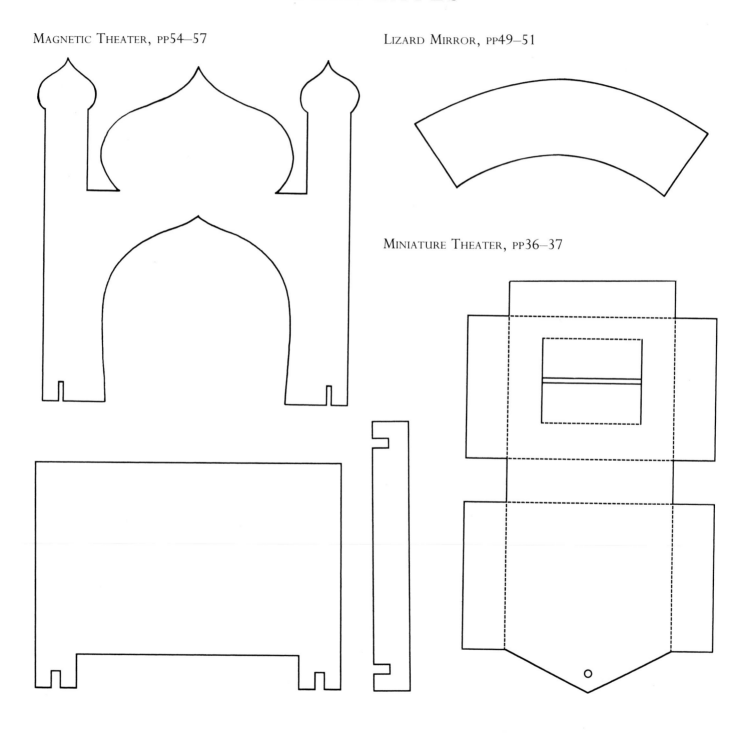